'Feck Off Depression'

About the Author

Seán O'Connor is a highly skilled and seasoned professional in the field of coaching and counselling. With many years of experience, Seán has made a significant impact on the lives of numerous individuals, guiding them towards personal growth, emotional well-being, and transformative change.

Throughout Seán's extensive career, he has honed his expertise in supporting clients from various backgrounds, facing diverse challenges, and seeking guidance in different areas of their lives. Whether it is professional development, relationship issues, mental health concerns, or personal transformation, Seán possesses the depth of knowledge and versatility to address a wide range of client needs.

As a coach, Seán brings a unique combination of empathy, active listening, and insightful questioning to help clients uncover their inner strengths, clarify their goals, and design effective strategies for achieving them. Seán is skilled at empowering individuals to overcome obstacles, embrace change, and unlock their full potential. With a supportive and non-judgmental approach, Seán fosters a safe space for clients to explore their thoughts, feelings, and aspirations, facilitating profound personal growth and self-discovery.

Furthermore, Seán excels as a counsellor, providing compassionate and evidence-based therapeutic interventions to individuals navigating challenging life circumstances.

His deep understanding of human psychology and emotional dynamics allows him to create a trusting therapeutic alliance, where clients feel heard, validated, and supported throughout their healing journey. Seán has successfully guided clients through trauma, grief, anxiety, depression, and other mental health challenges, equipping them with tools and coping strategies to regain their well-being and live fulfilling lives.

In addition to their extensive experience, Seán stays abreast of the latest research and best practices in coaching and counselling, continually enriching their knowledge and skills. He is committed to ongoing professional development and is dedicated to providing the highest standard of care to their clients.

Seán is known for their warmth, professionalism, and genuine passion for helping others. His ability to create a nurturing and empowering therapeutic environment allows clients to feel supported, validated, and inspired to embark on a transformative journey of self-discovery and growth.

In conclusion, Seán is a highly respected and experienced coach and counsellor, equipped with the wisdom, skills, and compassion to guide individuals towards personal transformation, emotional well-being, and empowered living.

Here's a quick rundown of Seán's publications to date:

A Therapist's Guide to a Little Bit of Everything: Is a comprehensive and invaluable resource designed to support therapists in navigating a wide range of topics and issues they may encounter in their practice.

Feck Off Anxiety: As someone deeply invested in the fields of Coaching and Counselling, I have witnessed firsthand the profound impact that anxiety can have on individuals, families, and communities.

Feck Off Stress: A guide that doesn't just help you cope with stress but empowers you to conquer it.

Feck Off Overthinking: Looks into the intricate web of overthinking, seeking not only to comprehend its depths but to provide you, the reader.

Leading in Healthcare Management and Leadership in the UK and Ireland: Exploring the intricacies of healthcare leadership and management, shedding light on effective practices in this ever-evolving field.

Leading with Purpose: A Guide to Being an Effective Chairperson in the Charity Sector of the UK and Ireland - Offering guidance to aspiring and current chairpersons, emphasizing the importance of purpose-driven leadership in the non-profit sector.

Empowering Voices: A Comprehensive Guide to Becoming a Freelance Contributor in Drug and Alcohol Addiction Journalism - A resource for aspiring freelance journalists interested in covering the crucial topics of drug and alcohol addiction.

Breaking the Chains: A Comprehensive Guide to Addiction Counselling in Ireland and the UK - Shedding light on effective counselling techniques and strategies to support individuals in overcoming addiction.

Shattering Stigma: This book aims to provide a comprehensive exploration of mental health services in Ireland, looking into the intricacies of assessment, diagnosis, and treatment.

Drive Aware: "Safer roads for a safer society" - This has been the driving principle behind the ambitious initiative known as the Drive Aware program in Ireland.

Empowering Change: A Project Manager's Perspective on the Disability Sector in Ireland: This comprehensive induction provides you with a strong foundation to navigate your role as a Project Manager in the disability sector.

Balancing Justice: A Magistrate's Journey - Sharing my personal experiences and insights as a magistrate, highlighting the challenges and rewards of serving in the legal system.

Mastering Life Coaching: A Comprehensive Guide for Professional Coaches - Equipping life coaches with the necessary tools and knowledge to empower their clients and facilitate positive change.

Clearing the Air: Smoking Cessation Services in the UK and their Benefits to Society - Advocating for the importance of smoking cessation and exploring the valuable services available to individuals looking to quit smoking.

Engineering Excellence: Unveiling the Potential of the Gas and Petroleum Industry' - An exploration of the gas and petroleum industry, revealing the incredible potential and advancements within this vital sector.

Plumbing for beginners: A Guide for Plumbers in the UK and Ireland. This book is specifically designed to provide aspiring plumbers, and plumbing enthusiasts in the United Kingdom and Ireland.

All of the above publications can be found at

https://www.amazon.co.uk/~/e/B0C8G4ZN94

Where you can contact him

Seán O'Connor Coaching

https://www.seanoconnorcoaching.com/

Drive Aware Ireland

https://www.driveaware.ie/

Table of Contents:

Introduction

In the grand tapestry of human existence, we find threads of joy and sorrow, love and pain, and the spectrum of emotions that define our shared journey. At the heart of this intricate weave lies a universal experience that touches the lives of millions, transcending age, race, and social standing. It is an experience that casts shadows on the brightest days and seems to whisper in the silence of the darkest nights. This experience is depression.

Depression is a formidable foe, a silent adversary that can take root in the human psyche, and if left unchecked, it can exert a pervasive influence over one's thoughts, emotions, and actions. Its reach extends far beyond the individual, affecting relationships, families, communities, and society at large. Yet, amid the shadowed valleys of despair, there is hope, for the journey to understanding and overcoming depression is one that countless individuals embark upon every day. It is a journey marked by resilience, self-discovery, and the unwavering belief that healing is not only possible but essential.

The Silent Intruder

Depression often arrives uninvited, akin to a silent intruder that slips through the back door of our consciousness. At first, its presence may be subtle, manifesting as a vague sense of unease or restlessness. Yet, as it settles in, its influence becomes more pronounced, casting a shadow over every facet of life. Its symptoms are as diverse as the individuals it afflicts, encompassing emotional, cognitive, and physical dimensions.

This book will look into the complex landscape of depression, unravelling its many facets and providing insights into its various forms, from major depressive disorder and persistent depressive disorder to the cyclical highs and lows of bipolar disorder.

We will explore the factors that can contribute to depression, including life events, childhood trauma, chronic stress, and the interplay between mental and physical health.

Seeking Help

In the darkest hours of depression, seeking help is the beacon of recovery. Yet, reaching out can be one of the most challenging and courageous steps on the journey to healing. We will discuss the importance of breaking the silence surrounding depression, dismantling the stigma that often shrouds it, and fostering open conversations about mental health.

Professional support plays a pivotal role in the healing process, and we will explore the various treatment options available, from psychotherapy and medication to alternative therapies and self-help strategies. Understanding the role of biological factors, neurotransmitters, and genetic predisposition will provide a comprehensive perspective on the science of depression.

Resources for Understanding and Healing

To further aid your journey, this book provides a wealth of resources, from worksheets and exercises for self-reflection to a glossary of terms and a comprehensive list of references and citations for those seeking deeper understanding.

The journey to understanding and overcoming depression is marked by both its challenges and its triumphs. It is a journey in which knowledge, compassion, and support are invaluable companions. With this book, you are not alone on this path, and together, we illuminate the way forward. The destination is healing, the journey is transformative, and the promise is that understanding and overcoming depression are not merely goals but a testament to the indomitable strength of the human spirit.

The Enigma of Depression

Depression, much like the ocean's depths, holds secrets hidden beneath its surface. At its core, it is not a fleeting melancholy but a profound and enduring state of despair. It is a mental tempest characterized by an overwhelming sense of desolation, the erosion of joy, and a disconnection from the very essence of life. In our quest to understand and conquer it, we must first unveil its true nature.

The Universal Struggle

Why does depression matter? It matters because it is a silent global epidemic. It matters because it affects humanity indiscriminately. From the bustling streets to the quiet corners of small towns, it touches lives without prejudice. It affects individuals regardless of their age, gender, race, or social status. By acknowledging this, we recognize that depression is not a weakness but a human struggle, and its impact reverberates throughout our communities, workplaces, and homes.

This book will guide you through the labyrinth of depression. It is a testament to the power of knowledge and resilience. We embark on a journey that encompasses the scientific, the emotional, and the practical. We will explore the intricate web of causation, the biology of the brain, and the myriad forms depression can assume.

We will look into the art of diagnosis, the diverse paths of treatment, and the art of self-help. We will listen to the voices of those who have faced this tempest and triumphed.

Embracing Hope

Amidst the profound challenges that depression poses, there is hope. This book is not just about the darkness but the journey towards the light.

It is about the strength that can be found within, the support that can be sought, and the strategies that can be employed to transcend depression's grasp. Through understanding, empathy, and resilience, we can confront depression and reclaim our lives.

Chapter 1

The Complexity of Depression

Depression is not merely a fleeting emotion or momentary sadness. It is a complex and multifaceted mental health condition that extends far beyond transitory melancholy. At its core, depression is characterized by a pervasive and long-lasting state of despair that goes well beyond what is considered a "bad day." It is akin to an enduring state of darkness that envelops the mind, robbing individuals of their vitality and affecting their overall well-being.

Individuals grappling with depression experience a persistent sense of sadness, often accompanied by feelings of worthlessness and guilt. Their emotional landscape resembles a desolate wasteland, devoid of colour or vibrancy. In this state, the horizon appears perpetually overcast, making it challenging to envision a brighter future.

The Cognitive Labyrinth

Depression's impact is not confined to emotional turmoil. It infiltrates the cognitive realms of the affected individuals. Thoughts become distorted, and the mind is often plagued by a relentless negative narrative. Self-doubt, self-criticism, and pervasive pessimism become frequent companions in the cognitive labyrinth of depression. It's a world where the mind becomes an echo chamber for self-critical and self-defeating thoughts.

This chapter look into the intricacies of these cognitive distortions, shedding light on how they contribute to the labyrinthine nature of depression. Understanding these cognitive aspects is vital because they often perpetuate the emotional distress and hinder the individual's ability to see a way out of the darkness.

The Physical Manifestations

Depression is not confined to the emotional and cognitive dimensions; it also manifests itself physically. Sleep disturbances, changes in appetite, and a pervasive lack of energy are common physical symptoms of depression. The body, much like the mind, becomes a battleground where depression exerts its influence.

Understanding these physical symptoms is crucial for a comprehensive grasp of the condition because they contribute to the overall burden of living with depression. Sleep disturbances, for example, can exacerbate emotional distress, while changes in appetite can lead to further physical and emotional health challenges. Recognizing the physical impact of depression is an essential part of addressing the condition.

The Persistence of Depression

Depression is characterized by its persistence. It differs from transient emotions or fleeting states of mind. While sadness or temporary emotional shifts are part of the human experience, depression endures over extended periods, often spanning weeks, months, or even years. Recognizing the chronic nature of depression is essential for diagnosing and effectively addressing the condition.

It is crucial to grasp that depression is not something that one can simply "snap out of" or overcome with a change in mindset. Acknowledging its persistent nature is the first step in understanding the depth of the challenge it presents.

The Multifaceted Nature

The multifaceted nature of depression demands a comprehensive understanding. It is not a one-size-fits-all condition. Rather, it takes various forms and intensities. Major depressive disorder, persistent depressive disorder, and bipolar depression are just a few examples of how depression can manifest differently in individuals.

Each form of depression may present unique challenges, symptoms, and treatment considerations. Understanding this diversity is essential for tailoring effective interventions and support to the specific needs of individuals.

Beyond Definition: A Teaser of What's to Come

While this chapter has laid the foundation by defining depression, it is important to remember that this definition, though crucial, is only the beginning of our journey. The pages ahead will unveil the intricate web that connects depression to our humanity. We will explore its causes, impact, and the myriad paths toward understanding and conquering this formidable foe.

This comprehensive book is designed to offer insights that illuminate the path toward healing and hope. It goes beyond mere definition, delving into the intricacies of depression and providing a holistic understanding of this complex and pervasive condition.

A Global Epidemic

Depression is a global epidemic that knows no boundaries. It transcends geographic, cultural, and demographic differences, affecting millions of lives across the world. This chapter seeks to underscore the universality of depression, emphasizing that it is not confined to any specific group, age, gender, or social status. Its prevalence on a global scale is a stark reminder that depression is a collective challenge, one that society must address together.

The global reach of depression highlights its significance, making it a concern that extends far beyond individual experiences. Recognizing its ubiquity encourages societies and individuals to confront this condition with empathy, understanding, and a commitment to finding solutions.

The Human Struggle

At its core, depression matters because it is an integral part of the human struggle. It is not a sign of weakness or moral failing, but rather, a shared experience among humankind. It is a mental tempest that can affect anyone, regardless of their resilience or strength. Understanding the universality of this struggle diminishes the stigma surrounding depression.

Acknowledging that depression is a part of the human experience fosters compassion and empathy. It reminds us that no one is immune to the challenges of mental health, and it encourages individuals to seek help without shame.

By recognizing the commonality of this struggle, society can work toward creating environments that support those facing depression.

The Ripple Effect

Depression extends its influence far beyond the individual who experiences it. In homes, workplaces, and communities, the ripple effect of depression is tangible. Relationships are strained, productivity wanes, and communities bear the burden of untreated depression. Depression disrupts the social fabric and underscores the importance of collective awareness and action.

The ripple effect of depression is a vital aspect of why it matters. It showcases that depression is not an isolated concern but a societal one. The strain it places on relationships and productivity highlights the urgent need for comprehensive support systems and treatment options. Addressing depression is not only an individual endeavour but a collective responsibility to restore the social fabric.

The Economic Toll

Beyond its emotional toll, depression carries a significant economic burden. Absenteeism and decreased productivity in the workplace, coupled with the costs of healthcare and treatment, represent a substantial financial strain. Recognizing the economic ramifications of depression highlights the urgency of addressing it effectively.

The economic toll of depression underscores because it matters not only from a humanitarian perspective but also from a practical one. The financial impact on workplaces and healthcare systems is substantial. Addressing depression isn't just about compassion; it's also a cost-effective strategy that can lead to increased productivity and reduced healthcare expenses. Acknowledging this economic aspect encourages policymakers, employers, and healthcare providers to invest in solutions for depression.

The Impetus for Change

The recognition of depression's pervasive impact serves as an impetus for change. By understanding its profound significance, we are motivated to confront depression head-on. It compels us to seek out solutions, raise awareness, and create supportive environments that facilitate recovery and healing.

The significance of depression as a catalyst for change cannot be understated. It propels societies, institutions, and individuals to take action. It fuels the drive to improve mental health care, reduce stigma, and establish accessible support systems.

By acknowledging the impetus for change, we acknowledge that depression matters because it inspires us to do better and create a more compassionate, understanding, and resilient world.

A Call for Empathy and Compassion

As we look into the significance of depression, we realize that it calls for empathy and compassion. The societal response to this condition must be one of understanding and support, not judgment.

Depression matters because it calls for a transformation in societal attitudes and responses. It requires a shift from judgment to empathy, from isolation to support.

Recognizing the call for empathy and compassion underscores the importance of addressing this condition not only through medical and therapeutic means but through a fundamental change in how society perceives and supports individuals facing depression.

A Glimpse of the Journey Ahead

This chapter sets the stage for the journey that lies ahead. It teases the exploration of depression's intricacies, from its biological underpinnings to the practical strategies for overcoming it. As we continue, we do so with the understanding that depression matters deeply, and it is a shared responsibility to address this complex and pervasive condition.

By providing a glimpse of the journey ahead, we prepare the reader for the comprehensive exploration of depression in the subsequent chapters. It emphasizes that understanding depression is not just a matter of academic or clinical interest but a profound journey that touches the lives of countless individuals. It sets the tone for a holistic and empathetic approach to understanding and addressing depression.

Chapter 2: The Science of Depression

To truly understand and overcome depression, it's essential to unravel the intricate science that underlies this condition. We will embark on a journey through the biological and neurological aspects of depression, shedding light on the complex factors that contribute to its onset.

The Brain in Turmoil

At the heart of depression lies a brain in turmoil. We look into the neurobiology of depression, exploring how imbalances in neurotransmitters disrupt communication within the brain. These neurotransmitters, including serotonin, norepinephrine, and dopamine, serve as chemical messengers, regulating mood and emotions. Imbalances in these crucial neurotransmitters can lead to emotional turbulence and are central to understanding the biological basis of depression.

Additionally, we explore the intricate feedback mechanisms in the brain, such as neurotransmitter reuptake. This process involves the reabsorption of neurotransmitters by nerve cells and can be disrupted in depression. Antidepressant medications aim to modify this process, restoring the balance of neurotransmitters and, in turn, alleviating depressive symptoms.

The Role of Genetics

Genetics also plays a crucial role in the development of depression. Genetic predisposition can increase an individual's vulnerability to this condition.

The inheritance of specific genes and variations can influence neurotransmitter function, stress response, and an individual's susceptibility to depression. These genetic factors often explain why depression may run in families, highlighting the genetic legacy of the condition.

The Stress Connection

Chronic stress is often a precursor to depression, and it triggers a cascade of physiological changes in the body. We will examine the role of the hypothalamic-pituitary-adrenal (HPA) axis, a central component of the body's stress response system.

Prolonged and excessive stress can lead to alterations in the structure and function of the brain, particularly in regions such as the prefrontal cortex and the hippocampus, which are implicated in emotional regulation and memory. These structural changes contribute to the development of depressive symptoms, making stress a significant factor in the biology of depression.

The Inflammation Puzzle

Recent research has uncovered a link between inflammation and depression, opening a new chapter in our understanding of the condition.

This role of pro-inflammatory cytokines, molecules involved in the body's immune response, and their potential influence on mood disorders. Inflammation within the brain is increasingly recognized as a contributing factor to depression, with high levels of pro-inflammatory cytokines being associated with depressive symptoms. Understanding the inflammatory aspect of depression offers new avenues for treatment and prevention, as anti-inflammatory interventions are being explored as potential therapies for depression.

Brain Structures and Depression

The brain is a complex landscape of interconnected structures, each playing a crucial role in emotional and cognitive processes. Regions like the prefrontal cortex, amygdala, and hippocampus are involved in depression. Changes in these brain areas are associated with various symptoms, such as emotional dysregulation and memory deficits. For example, a smaller hippocampus has been observed in individuals with depression, which may contribute to difficulties in memory and the processing of emotions.

Understanding the impact of depression on these brain structures is essential for comprehending the neurological underpinnings of the condition.

Neuroplasticity and Recovery

The brain's remarkable ability to change, known as neuroplasticity, offers a glimmer of hope in the understanding of depression.

Interventions like psychotherapy and medication can promote positive changes in the brain. Psychotherapy, such as cognitive-behavioural therapy, can lead to structural and functional changes in the brain that are associated with symptom improvement. Medications, particularly antidepressants, can also influence neuroplasticity, aiding in the recovery from depression. Understanding these neuroplastic changes highlights the potential for recovery and healing in individuals experiencing depression.

The Holistic View

Depression's science is not isolated; it's intertwined with the broader context of an individual's life. We emphasize the need to view the biological aspects of depression within a holistic framework, considering the influence of social, psychological, and environmental factors. The biology of depression does not operate in isolation; it interacts with an individual's life experiences, stressors, and support systems. This holistic perspective is crucial for a comprehensive understanding of depression.

Beyond the Biology

Understanding the science of depression is just the beginning of our journey. As we proceed, we'll explore how these biological insights are translated into practical strategies for diagnosis, treatment, and prevention.

By comprehending the intricate biology of depression, we are better equipped to navigate its complexities and chart a course toward healing and resilience.

Chapter 3: Types of Depression

Depression is a complex and multifaceted mental health condition. It doesn't manifest in a uniform manner but instead comes in various forms, each with its own unique characteristics and nuances. We will look into the diverse landscape of depression, offering insights into four prominent types: Major Depressive Disorder (MDD), Persistent Depressive Disorder (PDD), Bipolar Disorder, and Seasonal Affective Disorder (SAD).

Major Depressive Disorder (MDD)

Major Depressive Disorder is often considered the quintessential form of depression, characterized by a classic descent into darkness. Those with MDD often experience overwhelming and persistent sadness, often described as a heavy emotional burden that engulfs them. Loss of interest or pleasure in once-enjoyed activities is a hallmark feature, leaving individuals with a pervasive sense of emptiness. Beyond these emotional symptoms, MDD frequently entails a myriad of physical and cognitive manifestations.

The physical symptoms may include changes in sleep patterns, appetite, and energy levels. Sleep disturbances can manifest as insomnia or hypersomnia, leading to fatigue and a sense of physical exhaustion. Changes in appetite may result in weight gain or loss. Cognitive symptoms often involve difficulties with concentration and memory, making even simple tasks feel overwhelmingly challenging.

Diagnosis and Criteria

The diagnosis of MDD is a structured and clinical process guided by specific criteria outlined in psychiatric guidelines, typically the Diagnostic and Statistical Manual of Mental Disorders (DSM-5). These criteria include the presence of specific symptoms such as low mood, loss of interest, and changes in appetite or sleep patterns, among others, for a specific duration. Understanding these diagnostic criteria is crucial as they help mental health professionals differentiate between clinical depression and transient emotional states.

An accurate diagnosis is the first step toward effective treatment and support. It ensures that individuals with MDD receive the appropriate care and interventions necessary for managing their condition. Highlighting the importance of a proper diagnosis serves to destigmatize depression and encourage individuals to seek professional help when needed.

Persistent Depressive Disorder (PDD)

Persistent Depressive Disorder, also known as dysthymia, presents a unique and often challenging form of depression. Unlike MDD, which typically occurs in distinct episodes, PDD is characterized by its enduring nature.

It's akin to a constant companion, with symptoms persisting for an extended period, often measured in years rather than weeks or months. This unrelenting struggle can be particularly debilitating as individuals may become accustomed to a baseline of sadness and emotional suffering.

Living with PDD means carrying the burden of depression day in and day out, which can lead to feelings of hopelessness and a pervasive sense of unhappiness. Recognizing the chronic nature of PDD is pivotal for effective intervention and support, as it underscores the importance of addressing long-term depressive symptoms.

The Cumulative Burden

The cumulative burden of PDD is an aspect that sets it apart from other forms of depression. While some individuals may experience intermittent episodes of severe depression, those with PDD endure ongoing, milder symptoms that gradually erode self-esteem and overall functioning. Over time, the persistent nature of PDD can lead to a diminished sense of self-worth and affect various aspects of an individual's life, including their relationships, work, and overall quality of life.

Understanding the cumulative burden of PDD highlights the necessity of early intervention and ongoing support. Recognizing the insidious nature of this condition is the first step in breaking the cycle of chronic depression and helping individuals regain their emotional well-being.

Bipolar Disorder

Bipolar Disorder stands out as a unique and complex form of depression, characterized by distinct cycles of mood. It presents a rollercoaster of emotions, featuring two contrasting poles: mania and depression. During the manic phase, individuals often experience heightened energy, grandiosity, and a reduced need for sleep. They may engage in risky behaviours and have racing thoughts.

In contrast, the depressive phase is marked by symptoms similar to those seen in MDD, including profound sadness, loss of interest, and changes in appetite and sleep patterns.

The mood swings in Bipolar Disorder can be particularly challenging to manage, and recognizing these unique characteristics is crucial for an accurate diagnosis and effective treatment.

Diagnosis and Subtypes

Bipolar Disorder comes in various subtypes, each with its distinct pattern of mood episodes. Bipolar I Disorder involves manic episodes that may or may not be accompanied by depressive episodes. Bipolar II Disorder features depressive and hypomanic episodes. Cyclothymic Disorder entails numerous hypomanic and depressive symptoms but doesn't meet the diagnostic criteria for full-blown episodes.

Rapid-cycling Bipolar Disorder is characterized by four or more mood episodes in a year, a challenging subtype that requires careful management.

Accurate diagnosis is essential for tailoring treatment and support to the unique needs of individuals with Bipolar Disorder.

Seasonal Affective Disorder (SAD)

Seasonal Affective Disorder is a unique form of depression closely tied to specific seasons, with winter being the most common trigger. This condition often begins in the late fall or early winter and remits in the spring or early summer.

Individuals with SAD experience recurrent depressive episodes that align with the changing seasons, with mood improvements during sunnier months.

The seasonality of SAD has a significant impact on mood and behaviour. Those affected may experience low energy, a desire to oversleep, and cravings for carbohydrates, leading to weight gain. Light therapy, a common treatment modality, involves exposure to bright artificial light that mimics natural sunlight.

Understanding the connection between environmental changes and depressive symptoms is pivotal for managing SAD effectively.

Understanding the Circadian Rhythm

SAD is intimately tied to disruptions in the circadian rhythm, the body's internal biological clock that regulates sleep-wake cycles and other physiological processes. Reduced daylight hours in the winter months can lead to shifts in the circadian rhythm, affecting an individual's sleep patterns and overall mood.

We look into the mechanisms of how reduced daylight hours can disrupt the circadian rhythm, leading to depressive symptoms. It emphasizes the significance of addressing the biological clock in managing SAD, highlighting the potential for interventions that target these circadian disruptions.

A Holistic Perspective

Understanding the diverse types of depression is pivotal in tailoring effective interventions and support. This chapter illustrates that depression is not a one-size-fits-all condition.

By recognizing the unique features and challenges of MDD, PDD, Bipolar Disorder, and SAD, we pave the way for a more nuanced and effective approach to diagnosis, treatment, and support. The journey of understanding and overcoming depression begins with recognizing these distinct landscapes within the broader terrain of this condition.

Chapter 4: Causes and Triggers

Depression's genesis is a complex interplay of factors, some intrinsic, others external. In this chapter, we explore the multifaceted causes and triggers of depression, shedding light on how life events, childhood trauma, chronic stress, and medical conditions can contribute to the onset and progression of this condition.

Life Events: The Shaping of Experience

Life is a tapestry woven with various experiences, both joyful and challenging, that shape an individual's emotional landscape. Major life events, such as the loss of a loved one, relationship difficulties, or significant transitions like job changes or relocations, can have a profound impact on mental health. We look into the significance of these events in precipitating depressive episodes, emphasizing the diverse ways they can influence an individual's emotional state.

Vulnerability and Resilience

Not all individuals respond to life events in the same way. We explore the factors that render some more vulnerable to depression in the face of adversity, while others exhibit resilience. These factors can include personal coping strategies, social support systems, and genetic predispositions.

A nuanced understanding of these dynamics emphasizes the importance of personalized interventions, recognizing that one size does not fit all when it comes to addressing the impact of life events on mental health.

Childhood Trauma: Echoes of the Past

Childhood experiences can leave indelible marks on an individual's emotional well-being. This section looks into the profound impact of childhood trauma, such as abuse, neglect, or the loss of a caregiver, and how these early experiences can reverberate into adulthood. The enduring effects of childhood trauma increase the risk of depression in later life, highlighting the importance of addressing early-life experiences in the context of mental health.

Resilience and Recovery

While the echoes of childhood trauma can be enduring, resilience and recovery are possible. We will look at the potential for healing and highlights the role of therapeutic interventions, such as trauma-focused therapy, in addressing the wounds of the past. Recognizing that individuals can overcome the impact of childhood trauma through support and evidence-based treatments offers hope and a path toward emotional well-being.

Chronic Stress: A Pervasive Burden

Chronic stress is a persistent backdrop in the modern world, contributing to a pervasive burden on mental health.

We examine the intricate relationship between chronic stress and depression, delving into how prolonged exposure to stressors can wear down an individual's resilience and contribute to the onset of depression.

Chronic stress can trigger a cascade of physiological responses, including the release of stress hormones like cortisol, which can affect mood regulation.

Coping Strategies and Support

In the face of chronic stress, coping strategies and support systems play a pivotal role in maintaining mental health. This section explores the importance of developing adaptive ways of managing stress, such as mindfulness, exercise, and relaxation techniques. Additionally, fostering social connections and seeking support from friends, family, or mental health professionals can serve as a buffer against the impact of chronic stress. Recognizing that individuals have the capacity to develop effective stress management strategies and seek support emphasizes the role of resilience in mitigating the impact of stress on mental health.

Medical Conditions: The Intricate Interplay

Depression rarely exists in isolation from other medical conditions. We introduce the biopsychosocial model, which underscores the interplay between biological factors, psychological influences, and social context in the context of medical conditions that can trigger or exacerbate depressive symptoms.

This model emphasizes the multifaceted nature of depression, recognizing that it arises from a combination of physiological, psychological, and social factors.

The Role of Chronic Illness

Chronic illnesses such as diabetes, cancer, and heart disease can be both a cause and consequence of depression. We explore how these conditions may initiate depressive episodes through factors like pain, disability, and changes in body image. Simultaneously, depression can complicate the management of chronic illnesses, making it challenging for individuals to adhere to treatment plans and engage in self-care. Understanding the bidirectional relationship between depression and chronic illness is crucial for providing holistic care and improving overall well-being.

A Holistic Perspective

Understanding the causes and triggers of depression is a critical aspect of intervention and prevention. This chapter illustrates that depression is not solely an internal struggle but is intimately tied to external factors and experiences. By recognizing the profound impact of life events, childhood trauma, chronic stress, and medical conditions, we set the stage for a comprehensive approach to addressing depression. The journey to understanding and overcoming depression begins with acknowledging the diverse terrain from which it can emerge.

Chapter 5: Causes and Triggers

The genesis of depression is a complex interplay of factors, some intrinsic, others external. In this chapter, we look into deeper into the multifaceted causes and triggers of depression, shedding light on how life events, childhood trauma, chronic stress, and medical conditions can contribute to the onset and progression of this condition.

Life Events: The Shaping of Experience

Life events, whether positive or challenging, hold the power to mold an individual's emotional landscape. The significance of life events in precipitating depressive episodes is profound. Loss, relationship difficulties, job changes, and major life transitions can disrupt an individual's emotional equilibrium. The emotional toll of these experiences often leads to overwhelming sadness, anxiety, and an array of physical and cognitive symptoms. The unpredictability of life events underscores the diverse ways in which they can affect an individual's mental health. Understanding the connection between life events and depression highlights the importance of providing support during times of transition and difficulty.

Vulnerability and Resilience

Individuals vary in their response to life events. While some may be more vulnerable to depression when faced with adversity, others exhibit resilience, showing the ability to bounce back even in challenging circumstances. Factors contributing to vulnerability or resilience encompass personal coping strategies, social support systems, and genetic predispositions.

The interplay of these factors is complex and underscores that one's susceptibility to depression is not solely determined by external events. Recognizing the role of vulnerability and resilience allows for a more tailored approach to mental health support, with a focus on building coping skills and enhancing social connections.

Childhood Trauma: Echoes of the Past

Childhood experiences can cast long shadows on an individual's emotional well-being. Childhood trauma, such as physical or emotional abuse, neglect, or the loss of a caregiver, can have enduring effects on mental health. These early experiences shape an individual's psychological landscape, increasing the risk of depression in adulthood. The trauma experienced during childhood can lead to distorted beliefs about self-worth, trust issues, and emotional dysregulation. Understanding the legacy of childhood trauma emphasizes the necessity of addressing these wounds to promote mental well-being.

Resilience and Recovery

While childhood trauma can have lasting effects, resilience and recovery are possible. Many individuals who have experienced childhood trauma find healing and restoration through therapeutic interventions.

Trauma-focused therapies, such as cognitive-behavioural therapy (CBT) and eye movement desensitization and reprocessing (EMDR), have shown efficacy in helping individuals process and overcome traumatic experiences.

Recognizing that healing is achievable provides hope and reinforces the importance of accessible and evidence-based mental health services.

Chronic Stress: A Pervasive Burden

Chronic stress is a persistent presence in the modern world, contributing to a pervasive burden on mental health. The intricate relationship between chronic stress and depression involves the prolonged exposure to stressors that wear down an individual's resilience. Chronic stress can trigger a cascade of physiological responses, including the release of stress hormones like cortisol, which can affect mood regulation. The cumulative impact of chronic stress often manifests in symptoms like persistent sadness, irritability, and physical health issues.

Coping Strategies and Support

In the face of chronic stress, coping strategies and support systems play a pivotal role in maintaining mental health. Developing adaptive ways to manage stress, such as mindfulness, exercise, and relaxation techniques, can mitigate the impact of chronic stress. Equally important is the role of social connections and support from friends, family, or mental health professionals. These connections serve as a buffer against the detrimental effects of chronic stress. Recognizing the potential for individuals to develop effective stress management strategies and seek support emphasizes the role of resilience in mitigating the impact of stress on mental health.

Medical Conditions: The Intricate Interplay

Depression rarely exists in isolation from other medical conditions. The biopsychosocial model provides a framework that underscores the intricate interplay between biological factors, psychological influences, and social context in the context of medical conditions that can trigger or exacerbate depressive symptoms. This model emphasizes the multifaceted nature of depression, recognizing that it arises from a combination of physiological, psychological, and social factors.

The Role of Chronic Illness

Chronic illnesses, such as diabetes, cancer, and heart disease, can be both a cause and consequence of depression. These conditions may initiate depressive episodes through factors like pain, disability, and changes in body image. Simultaneously, depression can complicate the management of chronic illnesses, making it challenging for individuals to adhere to treatment plans and engage in self-care. Understanding the bidirectional relationship between depression and chronic illness is crucial for providing holistic care and improving overall well-being. Recognizing that individuals with chronic illnesses require comprehensive support, both for their physical health and emotional well-being, underscores the importance of an integrated approach to healthcare.

A Holistic Perspective

Understanding the causes and triggers of depression is a critical aspect of intervention and prevention. This chapter illustrates that depression is not solely an internal struggle but is intimately tied to external factors and experiences. By recognizing the profound impact of life events, childhood trauma, chronic stress, and medical conditions, we set the stage for a comprehensive approach to addressing depression.

The journey to understanding and overcoming depression begins with acknowledging the diverse terrain from which it can emerge.

Chapter 6: Symptoms and Diagnosis

Depression is a multifaceted condition, and recognizing its presence is pivotal for effective intervention. In this chapter, we explore the diverse symptoms of depression, categorized into emotional, cognitive, and physical domains, and look into the diagnostic process, highlighting the criteria and methods used for identifying depression.

Emotional Symptoms: The Hidden Storm

Emotional symptoms are often the most visible signs of depression, yet they reveal only the tip of the iceberg. Profound sadness, a pervasive feeling of despair that characterizes depression, extends beyond a temporary state of unhappiness. It manifests as an enduring emotional storm that clouds every aspect of life. Understanding the intensity and persistence of this sadness is crucial for recognizing and addressing depression. Individuals experiencing profound sadness may describe it as an emotional weight that makes even simple tasks seem insurmountable. This emotional burden can lead to emotional exhaustion, where even the smallest tasks can feel overwhelming.

Loss of Interest and Anhedonia

A hallmark feature of depression is the loss of interest in once-enjoyed activities. This loss extends to anhedonia, the inability to experience pleasure from activities that once brought joy. Anhedonia contributes to the emotional desolation of depression, leaving individuals feeling disconnected from the world around them.

Recognizing the absence of pleasure in activities that were once cherished is a key diagnostic indicator. Anhedonia can lead to social withdrawal and further isolation, as individuals may no longer find enjoyment in spending time with others.

Irritability and Anger

Emotions like irritability and anger are often overshadowed by profound sadness but are significant components of depressive symptomatology. These emotional states can manifest as outbursts of frustration, impatience, or even unexplained anger. Recognizing that irritability can be a hidden facet of depression is vital, as it can affect interpersonal relationships and lead to misunderstandings. Individuals with depression may find themselves easily triggered, leading to conflicts and a sense of guilt or shame about their emotional reactions.

Cognitive Symptoms: The Mind's Maze

Depression has a profound impact on cognition, leading to cognitive distortions. These distortions often accompany depressive episodes, resulting in negative thinking patterns, self-criticism, and rumination. Recognizing these cognitive distortions is essential for understanding the mental landscape of depression. Common distortions include catastrophizing, where individuals expect the worst possible outcomes, overgeneralization, where a single negative event is seen as a never-ending pattern, and dichotomous thinking, where situations are viewed in black-and-white terms.

These distortions can contribute to the maintenance of depressive symptoms and lead to a cycle of negative thinking.

Difficulty Concentrating and Making Decisions

The cognitive challenges of depression extend to difficulties in concentration and decision-making. Individuals with depression may struggle to focus on tasks, leading to reduced work or academic productivity.

Making even minor decisions can become an overwhelming process. Recognizing these cognitive impairments is vital for addressing the impact of depression on daily functioning. This difficulty in concentration can lead to feelings of incompetence and frustration, as individuals may find themselves unable to complete tasks they once managed easily.

Memory Impairment

Memory impairment is another cognitive symptom that is often underestimated. Depression can affect both short-term and long-term memory, leading to forgetfulness and lapses in memory. This can have consequences for work, personal relationships, and daily tasks. Individuals with depression may forget appointments, tasks, or important information, leading to a sense of frustration and self-blame. Recognizing memory impairment as a symptom of depression is crucial for an accurate diagnosis.

Physical Symptoms: The Body's Sighs

Physical symptoms of depression encompass sleep disturbances. These disturbances often manifest as insomnia, characterized by difficulty falling asleep or staying asleep, or hypersomnia, marked by excessive sleepiness. Sleep disturbances can impact energy levels and mood, exacerbating the emotional and cognitive symptoms of depression. Insomnia can lead to a sense of restlessness and exhaustion, while hypersomnia can result in excessive daytime sleepiness and difficulty in maintaining daily routines.

Changes in Appetite and Weight

Appetite changes, often leading to significant weight gain or loss, are common physical symptoms of depression. These changes result from complex psychobiological mechanisms and can have consequences for overall well-being.

Weight loss can lead to physical health concerns, while weight gain may contribute to self-esteem issues. Individuals with depression may lose interest in food or use it as a coping mechanism, leading to erratic eating patterns. Recognizing the relationship between appetite, weight, and depression is crucial for accurate diagnosis.

Fatigue and Low Energy

Fatigue and low energy levels are frequent complaints among individuals with depression. These physical symptoms can affect motivation and daily activities.

Fatigue often coexists with emotional and cognitive symptoms, contributing to the sense of physical and mental exhaustion that characterizes depression. Recognizing the presence of fatigue and low energy is essential for assessing the overall impact of depression on an individual's life. Individuals with depression may describe their energy levels as constantly depleted, making even routine tasks feel overwhelming.

Diagnosing Depression: The Clinical Portrait

The process of diagnosing depression is guided by specific criteria outlined in psychiatric manuals, such as the Diagnostic and Statistical Manual of Mental Disorders (DSM-5). These criteria include the duration and combination of symptoms required for a diagnosis. Recognizing the significance of these criteria is essential for an accurate and consistent identification of depression. Diagnosis typically requires the presence of specific symptoms over a specific duration, often two weeks or more, to distinguish depressive episodes from temporary emotional fluctuations.

The Clinical Interview

Diagnosis involves a clinical interview, where a healthcare professional assesses an individual's symptoms, their impact on daily life, and their duration. Open communication is paramount during this process, as it allows individuals to express their experiences and healthcare professionals to gain a comprehensive understanding of the individual's mental health.

The clinical interview is an opportunity for individuals to share their emotional, cognitive, and physical experiences, providing a holistic view of their mental state.

Self-Report Measures and Assessment Tools

In addition to clinical interviews, self-report measures and assessment tools are valuable in diagnosing depression. These tools include questionnaires and rating scales that quantify depressive symptoms and assess their severity. Utilizing such measures contributes to a more comprehensive and objective evaluation of depression. Self-report measures allow individuals to express their experiences in a structured format, helping healthcare professionals track changes in symptoms over time.

Differential Diagnosis

The diagnostic process also includes ruling out other medical and psychological conditions that may mimic depression. This differential diagnosis is crucial for ensuring the accurate identification of depression and the appropriate selection of treatment strategies. Other conditions, such as anxiety disorders, bipolar disorders, and medical conditions like hypothyroidism, can present with symptoms similar to depression. Accurate diagnosis is essential for tailoring treatment plans and interventions.

A Holistic Perspective

Symptoms and diagnosis are the gateway to understanding and addressing depression. This chapter illustrates the multifaceted nature of depression, emphasizing that it extends beyond emotional symptoms to encompass cognitive and physical domains. By recognizing the diverse clinical portrait of depression and the criteria used in its diagnosis, we set the foundation for effective intervention and support. The journey to understanding and overcoming depression begins with the clarity and accuracy of its diagnosis.

Chapter 7: The Impact of Depression

Depression is not confined to the realm of one's emotions; its effects reverberate through multiple facets of life. In this chapter, we explore the profound impact of depression on relationships, work and productivity, and physical health, shedding light on the complex interplay between this condition and the broader landscape of one's life.

Relationships: The Ripple Effect

Depression can cast a long, daunting shadow on family relationships. The emotional symptoms of depression, such as profound sadness and irritability, can strain family dynamics and create an atmosphere of tension. Loved ones may find it challenging to understand the changes in the individual with depression. Communication may break down, leading to a sense of isolation and frustration. The effects of depression ripple through the family, affecting not only the individual but also those closest to them. It's vital for family members to educate themselves about depression and seek support to navigate these challenges. Family therapy or support groups can be valuable resources.

Impact on Romantic Partnerships

Depression's impact on romantic relationships can be profound. The emotional turbulence that often accompanies depression can lead to misunderstandings and emotional distance between partners. The depressed individual may have difficulty expressing their feelings, and their partner may struggle to provide the support needed.

Open communication is crucial in navigating these challenges. Couples therapy can be a beneficial avenue for addressing issues stemming from depression and learning effective strategies for support and communication.

Social Isolation

Isolation is a common consequence of depression. Individuals with depression may withdraw from social activities and isolate themselves from friends and loved ones. The emotional exhaustion and persistent feelings of sadness can make social interactions feel overwhelming. The resultant loneliness can deepen the emotional burden of depression. Friends and family may find it challenging to reach out or understand the extent of the individual's isolation. Recognizing this isolation and offering support, even in small ways, can make a significant difference in the individual's journey toward recovery. Encouraging social engagement at a pace comfortable for the person with depression can be a helpful step.

Work and Productivity: The Professional Terrain

Depression often brings decreased work productivity. Cognitive impairments, including difficulties in concentration and memory, can significantly affect job performance. The individual may find it challenging to focus on tasks, leading to decreased efficiency and effectiveness. This can result in missed deadlines, errors, and increased work-related stress. Employers and colleagues can play a supportive role by understanding the impact of depression on work performance.

Flexible work arrangements, reasonable accommodations, and an empathetic work environment can go a long way in helping individuals with depression maintain their productivity.

Absenteeism and Job Loss

Depression can result in absenteeism and, in severe cases, job loss. The emotional and physical toll of depression may make it impossible for the individual to maintain regular attendance at work. Absenteeism can lead to financial strain, exacerbating feelings of worthlessness and hopelessness. Job loss can further compound the individual's emotional distress and economic instability. It's essential for individuals facing these challenges to seek support from mental health professionals, employee assistance programs, and legal advisors when necessary.

Workplace Stigma

Stigma surrounding mental health issues can create additional challenges in the workplace. Many individuals with depression hesitate to disclose their condition due to fear of discrimination or judgment. This section emphasizes the need for destigmatizing conversations around depression and the importance of creating supportive work environments. Employers should encourage open dialogue about mental health, provide mental health resources, and train managers and colleagues to recognize and support those experiencing depression. It's important to foster an inclusive and understanding work culture where individuals feel safe seeking help when needed.

Physical Health: The Body's Response

Depression can affect the immune system and increase inflammation in the body. This biological response may contribute to physical health issues, such as cardiovascular problems, diabetes, and autoimmune diseases. Chronic stress and inflammation can have long-term effects on the body's systems, leading to an increased risk of various health conditions. Recognizing the link between depression and physical health is crucial for holistic care and intervention. Healthcare providers should consider the physical health implications of depression when providing treatment, and individuals with depression should be encouraged to adopt a healthy lifestyle to mitigate these risks.

Sleep Disturbances and Health

The physical toll of depression includes sleep disturbances. Poor sleep quality, often observed in individuals with depression, can affect the body's immune function and increase the risk of various health conditions. Addressing sleep disturbances is an essential part of managing the physical health consequences of depression. Mental health professionals should explore sleep patterns with their clients and recommend strategies to improve sleep quality.

Self-Care and Well-Being

Depression often leads to self-neglect. Individuals with depression may struggle to engage in self-care practices, such as regular exercise, maintaining a balanced diet, and attending medical check-ups.

This section underscores the importance of self-care and well-being in managing the physical health consequences of depression. Encouraging individuals with depression to prioritize self-care can be a significant step in improving their overall well-being. Healthcare providers should work with individuals to create self-care plans tailored to their needs.

A Holistic Perspective

Understanding the impact of depression extends beyond its emotional toll. This chapter illustrates how depression's effects ripple through relationships, work, and physical health. By recognizing the intricate interplay between depression and these life domains, we set the stage for a comprehensive approach to addressing depression. The journey to understanding and overcoming depression begins with acknowledging the far-reaching impact it has on one's life and the importance of holistic support and intervention.

Chapter 8: Treatment Options

Addressing depression is a multifaceted journey, and treatment options provide a compass for navigating this challenging terrain. In this chapter, we explore a range of treatments, including psychotherapy, medication, and alternative therapies, highlighting their efficacy and the unique benefits they offer in the quest for healing and resilience.

Psychotherapy: Unravelling the Mind's Patterns

Cognitive Behavioural Therapy (CBT) is the cornerstone of psychotherapeutic treatment for depression. This form of therapy looks deep into the principles of CBT, emphasizing how it targets negative thought patterns and behaviours that contribute to depressive symptoms. CBT empowers individuals by providing them with practical strategies to recognize, challenge, and change their mental landscape. Through structured sessions, individuals learn to reframe negative thinking and develop healthier coping mechanisms, promoting lasting resilience against depression's grip. The therapist works collaboratively with the individual to set specific goals and develop skills to manage depressive symptoms effectively.

Interpersonal Therapy (IPT)

Interpersonal Therapy (IPT) takes a unique approach by focusing on the impact of relationships on one's mental health. This section explores how IPT helps individuals address relationship difficulties and unresolved conflicts, which can often be significant contributors to depressive symptoms.

IPT provides a supportive environment where individuals can explore and navigate their interpersonal challenges, improving their emotional well-being and strengthening their connections with others. By addressing relational issues, IPT aims to alleviate depressive symptoms and help individuals foster healthier, more fulfilling social connections.

Other Psychotherapies

Beyond CBT and IPT, a diverse array of other psychotherapies offers unique approaches to depression treatment. We look into therapies such as psychodynamic therapy, behavioural activation, and mindfulness-based cognitive therapy (MBCT) and their respective roles in depression treatment. Each of these therapies provides individuals with distinct tools and insights for managing and ultimately overcoming their depressive symptoms.

- Psychodynamic therapy explores the influence of past experiences and unconscious thoughts on current emotional struggles, offering individuals a chance to gain a deeper understanding of their inner world and how it relates to their depression.

- Behavioural activation focuses on helping individuals reengage in activities they have withdrawn from due to depression, encouraging a gradual return to a fulfilling and meaningful life.

- Mindfulness-based cognitive therapy (MBCT) combines mindfulness techniques with cognitive therapy to help individuals break the cycle of recurrent depression by becoming more aware of their thoughts and emotions.

The choice of psychotherapy may depend on an individual's personal preferences, specific symptoms, and therapeutic goals, highlighting the importance of tailoring treatment to the individual.

Medication: Balancing Brain Chemistry

Antidepressant Medications

Antidepressant medications play a pivotal role in treating depression. We discuss the various classes of antidepressants, including selective serotonin reuptake inhibitors (SSRIs), serotonin-norepinephrine reuptake inhibitors (SNRIs), and atypical antidepressants, highlighting their mechanisms of action in the brain and potential side effects. Antidepressants work by balancing the levels of neurotransmitters in the brain, such as serotonin and norepinephrine, which are essential for regulating mood. The choice of medication is often based on an individual's symptoms, medical history, and any previous responses to treatment.

- Selective serotonin reuptake inhibitors (SSRIs) are commonly prescribed as they are generally well-tolerated and have fewer side effects. They work by increasing the availability of serotonin in the brain.

- Serotonin-norepinephrine reuptake inhibitors (SNRIs) affect both serotonin and norepinephrine levels and are often prescribed for individuals with more severe symptoms.

- Atypical antidepressants have varied mechanisms of action and may be considered when other types of antidepressants are ineffective or cause unwanted side effects.

Mood Stabilizers

In cases of bipolar disorder, mood stabilizers are essential for regulating mood swings. This section explores mood-stabilizing medications like lithium and anticonvulsants, emphasizing their role in bipolar depression treatment. These medications help stabilize mood and prevent the oscillations between manic and depressive episodes in individuals with bipolar disorder, enabling them to achieve greater emotional stability.

- Lithium is a well-established mood stabilizer that can be effective in preventing both depressive and manic episodes.

- Anticonvulsant medications, such as valproic acid and lamotrigine, are also used to manage mood swings in bipolar disorder.

Augmentation and Combination Strategies

Combination treatments, involving both psychotherapy and medication, can be highly effective. We examine how augmenting treatment with different modalities can enhance outcomes for individuals with depression.

This approach acknowledges the multifaceted nature of depression, addressing it from both the psychological and neurochemical angles. The synergy between psychotherapy and medication offers individuals a more comprehensive and personalized path to recovery. By combining the skills and insights gained in therapy with the neurochemical support of medication, individuals can experience enhanced symptom relief and long-term resilience against depression.

Alternative Therapies: Holistic Approaches

Mindfulness and Meditation

Mindfulness and meditation offer individuals powerful tools for managing depressive symptoms. We explore how mindfulness practices can cultivate self-awareness, emotional regulation, and resilience. Mindfulness-based techniques encourage individuals to stay in the present moment, observing their thoughts and feelings without judgment. This can lead to a deeper understanding of one's emotional landscape and the development of healthier responses to stress and sadness. Regular mindfulness practice has been shown to reduce the recurrence of depressive episodes and improve overall well-being.

A Comprehensive Approach

In conclusion, adopting a lifestyle that promotes well-being can be a game-changer in managing depression. It's essential to recognize that these lifestyle changes don't replace professional treatment but can complement it.

Each person's journey to well-being is unique, but these practical changes in diet, exercise, sleep, and stress management can significantly impact mental health. Case studies illustrate how real individuals have incorporated these changes into their lives, resulting in improvements in their depressive symptoms.

By making informed choices and taking small, sustainable steps, individuals can harness the power of their daily habits to support their journey towards mental health and well-being. Remember, a brighter and healthier future is within reach.

A Holistic Perspective

The treatment of depression extends far beyond a one-size-fits-all approach. This chapter illustrates the diverse range of options available, emphasizing that what works best may vary from person to person. By recognizing the efficacy of psychotherapy, medication, and alternative therapies, we set the foundation for a comprehensive approach to addressing depression. The journey to understanding and overcoming depression is marked by a personalized treatment plan that respects an individual's unique needs, preferences, and goals.

Chapter 9: Self-Help Strategies

Beyond professional treatment, self-help strategies are a vital component of managing and overcoming depression. In this chapter, we explore the empowering world of self-help, highlighting the effectiveness of lifestyle changes, coping skills, and the role of support systems in the journey to healing and resilience.

Lifestyle and Depression

Depression is a complex condition influenced by a myriad of factors, and among them, our daily habits play a pivotal role. In this chapter, we will explore the profound connection between lifestyle choices and mental health. Understanding how diet, exercise, sleep, and stress management can affect depression can be a transformative step towards a healthier and happier life.

Diet

The saying "You are what you eat" couldn't be more accurate when it comes to mental health. Our diet not only nourishes our body but also impacts our brain and mood. Consider the following:

- Nutrient-Rich Foods: Foods rich in nutrients like omega-3 fatty acids, antioxidants, and B vitamins can support brain health. Example: Sarah adopted a diet rich in fish, leafy greens, and whole grains, and she noticed a significant improvement in her mood over time.

- The Gut-Brain Connection: Emerging research suggests a strong link between gut health and mental well-being. Probiotics and a diet that promotes a healthy gut microbiome can have a positive impact. Example: John incorporated probiotics and fibre-rich foods into his diet and noticed a reduction in depressive symptoms.

Exercise

Regular physical activity is not only essential for physical health but also plays a vital role in managing depression:

- Endorphin Release: Exercise triggers the release of endorphins, often referred to as "feel-good" hormones. Regular physical activity can elevate mood and reduce symptoms of depression. Example: Emma started a daily exercise routine, and over time, her depressive episodes became less frequent and less severe.

- Stress Reduction: Physical activity is a potent stress reliever. It helps reduce cortisol levels, the stress hormone, and promotes relaxation. Example: Mark incorporated yoga into his daily routine to manage stress, and he found it beneficial in reducing symptoms of depression.

Sleep

Sleep is an often-underestimated component of mental health:

- Sleep Quality: The quality of sleep is just as important as the quantity. Disrupted or insufficient sleep can worsen depressive symptoms. Example: Michael implemented a sleep schedule and established a calming bedtime routine, which significantly improved the quality of his sleep and reduced his depression.

- Sleep Hygiene: Practices like limiting screen time before bed, creating a comfortable sleep environment, and avoiding caffeine in the evening can contribute to better sleep. Example: Laura incorporated these practices into her life, resulting in more restful nights and improved mood.

Stress Management

Managing stress is critical in the context of depression:

- Mindfulness and Meditation: Mindfulness practices can help individuals become more aware of their thoughts and emotions and reduce rumination. Example: Alex engaged in daily mindfulness meditation and found it beneficial in managing stress and depression.

- Time Management: Effective time management and setting boundaries can reduce the overwhelming feeling that often accompanies depression.

Example: Jessica learned time management techniques, allowing her to balance work and personal life more effectively, reducing stress and depression.

Mindfulness and Meditation

Mindfulness and meditation offer practical tools for managing depressive symptoms. We explore how these practices cultivate self-awareness, emotional regulation, and resilience, making them valuable coping skills for individuals with depression. In this section, a comprehensive guide to practicing mindfulness and meditation is provided. Various techniques, such as mindfulness meditation, loving-kindness meditation, and body scan, are explained in detail, allowing individuals to choose the approach that resonates with them. The benefits of these practices, including improved emotional regulation and reduced rumination, are discussed with scientific evidence. Practical exercises for incorporating mindfulness and meditation into daily life are offered, enabling individuals to develop a regular practice that supports their mental health.

Mindfulness and Meditation Example: Meet Emily, who has been battling depression. She decided to incorporate mindfulness meditation into her daily routine. She practiced mindfulness by focusing on the present moment and observing her thoughts without judgment. Over time, Emily noticed a significant improvement in her emotional regulation and reduced rumination.

This example illustrates how mindfulness and meditation can be powerful tools for individuals in managing depressive symptoms.

Cognitive Restructuring

Cognitive restructuring involves challenging and reframing negative thought patterns. We discuss the principles of cognitive restructuring and how it empowers individuals to shift their mental landscape toward a more positive and adaptive outlook.

This section provides an in-depth exploration of cognitive restructuring, outlining the steps involved in identifying and challenging negative thought patterns. Examples illustrate how individuals have successfully applied cognitive restructuring to transform their thinking and improve their emotional well-being. Practical exercises and worksheets are included to guide individuals through the process of recognizing cognitive distortions and replacing them with more balanced and rational thoughts. This hands-on approach empowers individuals to take control of their thinking patterns and reduce the impact of negative thoughts on their mood.

Cognitive Restructuring Example: Consider Tom, who often struggled with negative thought patterns that exacerbated his depression. Tom learned cognitive restructuring techniques, which involved identifying and challenging these negative thoughts. By using practical exercises and worksheets, he replaced his cognitive distortions with more balanced and rational thoughts.

This process empowered Tom to take control of his thinking patterns, leading to improved emotional well-being.

Stress Reduction Techniques

Stress management is pivotal in the context of depression. We examine stress reduction techniques, such as deep breathing, progressive muscle relaxation, and time management, offering individuals strategies to alleviate stressors in their lives. In this section, a comprehensive toolbox of stress reduction techniques is presented. Deep breathing exercises are explained in detail, with guidance on various breathing techniques, such as diaphragmatic breathing and box breathing, to reduce physiological stress responses. Progressive muscle relaxation is explored, with step-by-step instructions for achieving physical and mental relaxation. Time management strategies, including prioritization and time-blocking, are covered to help individuals regain a sense of control over their daily schedules. Real-life examples of individuals who have effectively managed stress through these techniques are shared, providing inspiration and motivation.

Stress Reduction Techniques Example: Let's look at Sarah, who faced high stress levels that aggravated her depression. She adopted various stress reduction techniques, including deep breathing and time management strategies. Sarah practiced deep breathing exercises such as diaphragmatic breathing and box breathing to reduce physiological stress responses.

Additionally, she implemented time management techniques to prioritize tasks and regain control over her daily schedule. These strategies helped Sarah effectively manage her stress and contributed to her overall well-being.

Support Systems: Building a Resilient Network

Personal Relationships

Personal relationships are a vital source of support. We explore how open communication, empathy, and active listening can strengthen these connections and aid individuals in their battle against depression. This section looks into the intricacies of building and maintaining healthy personal relationships while managing depression. Strategies for open and honest communication are provided, along with practical tips for expressing one's needs and emotions effectively. The importance of empathy and active listening in strengthening relationships is emphasized, with guidance on developing these skills. Real-life stories of individuals who have navigated personal relationships successfully while coping with depression are shared to offer insights and encouragement.

Personal Relationships Example: Meet Sarah and Mark, a couple dealing with depression in their individual lives. They recognized the importance of open communication and empathy in their relationship. They began having regular, honest conversations about their feelings and needs. Both learned to actively listen and offer emotional support.

This strengthened their bond, making their relationship a source of resilience in their battle against depression. Their journey illustrates how nurturing healthy personal relationships can be a vital part of a support system.

Support Groups

Support groups offer individuals a sense of community and shared experience. We investigate how joining a support group can provide a platform for discussing challenges, gaining insights, and fostering hope. Various types of support groups, including in-person and online options, are discussed, allowing individuals to choose the format that suits their needs. The benefits of joining a support group, such as reducing feelings of isolation, sharing experiences, and gaining practical advice, are highlighted.

Support Groups Example: Consider Amy, who was feeling isolated and overwhelmed by her depression. She decided to join a local depression support group. In this group, she found a community of people who understood her struggles. They shared their experiences, offered practical advice, and provided emotional support. Being part of this support group reduced Amy's feelings of isolation and helped her regain a sense of hope. Her experience highlights the transformative power of shared experiences and the sense of belonging that support groups can provide.

Professional Help

Professional support is an essential element of any support system. We highlight the importance of continuing therapy or medication under the guidance of a mental health professional. The significance of professional mental health support is underscored, with a detailed examination of the role of therapists, psychiatrists, and other mental health professionals in the treatment of depression. Practical advice on finding the right mental health professional, establishing a therapeutic relationship, and maintaining effective communication is provided. The importance of continuing therapy or medication management under professional guidance is emphasized, ensuring that individuals receive the appropriate care and support for their unique needs.

Professional Help Example: Let's look at Tom, who had been receiving therapy for his depression. His therapist, Dr. Smith, played a crucial role in his treatment. Dr. Smith guided Tom in identifying and challenging negative thought patterns through cognitive restructuring. They established a therapeutic relationship based on trust and open communication. With Dr. Smith's support, Tom continued therapy and medication management, ensuring he received the appropriate care and support tailored to his unique needs. This example emphasizes the essential role of mental health professionals in the treatment of depression and the importance of continuing professional support.

These examples illustrate the significance of personal relationships, support groups, and professional help in building a resilient support system for managing depression

A Holistic Perspective

Self-help strategies empower individuals to take an active role in their journey to healing and resilience. This chapter illustrates the diverse range of self-help techniques available, emphasizing that what works best may vary from person to person. By recognizing the effectiveness of lifestyle changes, coping skills, and support systems, we set the foundation for a comprehensive and personalized approach to addressing depression.

The journey to understanding and overcoming depression is marked by the resilience and self-empowerment that individuals can cultivate on their path to well-being.

A Comprehensive Approach

In conclusion, adopting a lifestyle that promotes well-being can be a game-changer in managing depression. It's essential to recognize that these lifestyle changes don't replace professional treatment but can complement it.

Each person's journey to well-being is unique, but these practical changes in diet, exercise, sleep, and stress management and supports can significantly impact mental health.

By making informed choices and taking small, sustainable steps, individuals can harness the power of their daily habits to support their journey towards mental health and well-being. Remember, a brighter and healthier future is within reach.

Chapter 10: Preventing Depression

Prevention is a powerful strategy in the battle against depression. In this chapter, we explore the proactive measures individuals can take to prevent depression, focusing on building resilience and the significance of early intervention in preserving mental health.

Building Resilience: Fortifying the Mind

Resilience as a Shield

Resilience is the capacity to bounce back from adversity. We look into the concept of resilience, emphasizing its role as a protective shield against depression. Through examples, we demonstrate how resilience acts as a powerful shield against depression. It encompasses emotional strength, adaptability, and effective coping skills. Real-life examples of individuals who have faced significant challenges and emerged with increased resilience serve as inspiring models. We look into deeper into the science of resilience, explaining the neurological and psychological processes that underlie this trait.

Enhancing Resilience

Resilience is a trait that can be cultivated and strengthened. We explore how individuals can enhance their resilience through various means, including developing a positive mindset, practicing self-compassion, and nurturing social connections.

We will look into Evidence-based strategies are detailed for developing a positive mindset, including techniques for cultivating gratitude, optimism, and resilience-affirming self-talk. The role of self-compassion in resilience building is explored in depth, with practical exercises and real-world examples of individuals who have benefited from self-compassion practices. Strategies for building and nurturing social connections are presented, with a focus on fostering supportive relationships and networks that bolster resilience.

Early Life Resilience

Early life experiences play a pivotal role in shaping resilience. We investigate how fostering resilience in childhood can contribute to lifelong mental well-being, providing a foundation for preventing depression. In this section, we look into the critical importance of early life experiences in shaping resilience. Through example we explore how childhood experiences, both positive and adverse, can significantly impact an individual's ability to develop resilience. We provide practical guidance for parents, educators, and caregivers on how to promote resilience in children, including strategies for fostering emotional intelligence and effective stress coping skills.

Early Life Resilience Example: Meet Jenny, a child who grew up in a supportive and nurturing environment. Her parents and teachers encouraged her to express her emotions openly and provided guidance in managing stress and challenges. They emphasized the importance of emotional intelligence, teaching her to recognize and understand her feelings.

As Jenny progressed through her childhood, she faced various life experiences, including academic stress and occasional setbacks. However, her early exposure to a supportive and resilient mindset helped her navigate these challenges. She learned to approach setbacks with a positive attitude and view them as opportunities for growth.

Jenny's early life experiences, characterized by emotional support and the development of effective stress-coping skills, significantly contributed to her resilience. As she entered adulthood, she carried these skills with her, making her better equipped to face life's ups and downs. Her story illustrates how fostering resilience in childhood through emotional support and skill development can provide a strong foundation for lifelong mental well-being and the prevention of depression.

Early Intervention: Nipping Depression in the Bud

Early intervention hinges on recognizing the early warning signs of depression. We discuss these signs, such as persistent sadness, changes in sleep and appetite, and loss of interest in activities, highlighting the importance of seeking help when they emerge. In this section, we offer a comprehensive guide to recognizing the early warning signs of depression. Examples illustrate how subtle changes in mood, behaviour, and physical well-being can be early indicators of depression. We explore the range of emotional, cognitive, and physical symptoms to look out for. Strategies for maintaining a mood diary and utilizing self-assessment tools are discussed, enabling individuals to monitor their emotional well-being effectively.

Seeking Professional Support

Early intervention necessitates seeking professional support. We emphasize the significance of reaching out to mental health professionals when symptoms are still manageable, ensuring that individuals receive timely and effective treatment. In this section, we provide a thorough overview of the process of seeking professional help. Real-life testimonials from individuals who have benefited from early intervention highlight the importance of taking this step. Practical advice on how to find a suitable mental health professional, prepare for the initial appointment, and engage in open communication with providers is presented.

The benefits of early intervention in preserving mental well-being and preventing the progression of depression are emphasized, with evidence supporting the effectiveness of timely professional support.

Seeking Professional Support Example: Meet Alex, a young professional who had been noticing subtle but persistent changes in his mood and behaviour. He experienced a persistent feeling of sadness, had trouble sleeping, and found himself losing interest in activities he once enjoyed. Recognizing these early warning signs of depression, Alex decided to take proactive steps to seek professional help.

He started by researching mental health professionals in his area and found a therapist with expertise in depression. With some guidance, he prepared a list of his symptoms and concerns, which he planned to discuss during his initial appointment.

During his first session, Alex openly communicated his feelings and experiences to his therapist. They discussed his symptoms and worked together to develop an initial treatment plan, which included therapy and potential medication if necessary.

As Alex continued with his therapy sessions, he learned effective strategies to manage his depression and build resilience. With early intervention and the support of a mental health professional, he was able to prevent his depression from worsening and disrupting his life. Alex's story serves as an example of the importance of recognizing early warning signs and seeking professional support promptly to preserve mental well-being and prevent the progression of depression.

Education and Awareness

Educating oneself and others about depression is a proactive step in early intervention. We discuss the importance of mental health education and creating a culture of awareness that destigmatizes seeking help for emotional difficulties. We will look into the role of education and awareness in early intervention. We examine the far-reaching benefits of mental health literacy, not only in identifying depression but also in reducing stigma and promoting early intervention.

Strategies for mental health education in schools, workplaces, and communities are discussed, along with real-world examples of initiatives that have successfully raised awareness and created supportive environments. The significance of open, stigma-reducing conversations about mental health is emphasized, with guidance on how individuals can foster these discussions within their personal and professional circles.

Education and Awareness Example: Consider Sarah, a high school teacher who recognized the importance of mental health education in her school community. She was aware that many students and even some colleagues faced mental health challenges, including depression, but were often hesitant to seek help due to stigma.

Sarah took the initiative to introduce a mental health awareness program in her school. Working closely with the school administration and a local mental health organization, she organized workshops and presentations on mental health and depression. These sessions covered topics such as recognizing signs of depression, understanding the importance of seeking help, and reducing stigma around mental health issues.

The program also encouraged open conversations about mental health among students, teachers, and staff. Sarah and her colleagues shared personal stories of their own mental health journeys, which helped create a culture of empathy and support within the school community.

As a result of these efforts, more students and staff felt comfortable discussing their emotional difficulties and seeking help when needed. The school's mental health program not only increased awareness of depression but also reduced the stigma associated with it. Sarah's proactive approach in promoting education and awareness played a vital role in early intervention and preserving the mental well-being of her school community. This example illustrates how education and awareness initiatives can create supportive environments and encourage early intervention.

A Holistic Perspective

Preventing depression is a collective effort that begins with building resilience and embracing early intervention. This chapter illustrates that while prevention is a goal that extends beyond the scope of any individual, individuals can take proactive steps to safeguard their mental health.

By recognizing the power of resilience and the significance of early intervention, we set the stage for a culture of mental well-being and resilience. The journey to understanding and overcoming depression is marked not only by addressing its presence but by fostering a future where depression can be prevented and minimized.

Chapter 11: Depression in Different Age Groups

Depression does not discriminate by age; it can affect individuals across the lifespan. In this chapter, we look into the unique manifestations and considerations of depression in children, teenagers, and the elderly, offering comprehensive insights into how this condition can impact each age group.

Depression in Children: Navigating Young Emotions

Recognizing Childhood Depression

Depression in children often presents differently than in adults. We begin by shedding light on the nuanced signs and symptoms of childhood depression. Examples will provide valuable context for understanding how children may express their emotional distress. We explore how behaviours like irritability, somatic complaints (such as stomach-aches or headaches), and changes in school performance can serve as indicators. Furthermore, we provide parents, teachers, and caregivers with practical strategies for early detection, emphasizing the crucial role they play in recognizing and addressing childhood depression.

Causes and Risk Factors

To comprehensively understand childhood depression, we must consider its causes and risk factors. We look into the multifaceted nature of these factors, including genetic predisposition, family dynamics, and life stressors.

Treatment and Support

Treating childhood depression requires a sensitive and family-oriented approach. We investigate the effectiveness of various treatment modalities, with a focus on psychotherapy. Examples of children and their families navigating the challenges of childhood depression offer insights into the importance of early intervention. We discuss the role of parents, educators, and mental health professionals in providing the necessary support. Practical tips and guidance are included for parents and caregivers on how to communicate with and support a child struggling with depression. Additionally, we highlight the significance of a supportive community and offer insights into how schools and communities can contribute to the well-being of children.

Childhood Depression Example: Imagine a 10-year-old child named Sarah. Her parents start noticing that she's become increasingly irritable, and she frequently complains of stomach-aches before school. They also observe a decline in her academic performance. These are potential indicators of childhood depression.

Recognizing these signs early, Sarah's parents seek guidance from her school counsellor and a child psychologist. Through therapy and support, they help Sarah cope with her emotions and provide a nurturing environment to aid her recovery.

Teenage Depression: Navigating the Turbulent Years

The Unique Challenges of Adolescence

Teenage depression intersects with the tumultuous period of adolescence. We explore the distinct challenges that teenagers face, such as peer pressure, academic stress, and the quest for identity.

We look into the intricacies of brain development, hormonal changes, and emotional well-being in teenagers, offering insights into why this age group is particularly vulnerable to depression. Practical advice for parents and educators on how to provide support and navigate the complexities of teenage depression is included.

Warning Signs and Communication

Recognizing the warning signs of teenage depression is vital. We discuss how communication and open dialogue between parents, educators, and teenagers can bridge the gap and offer support. Strategies for parents and educators on creating a safe space for teenagers to express their emotions and seek help are explored, with an emphasis on the role of early intervention in ensuring the well-being of adolescents.

Prevention and Intervention

Preventing and intervening in teenage depression are proactive steps that can set the course for a lifetime of well-being. In this section, we explore how schools, communities, and mental health services can play a pivotal role in addressing the mental health of teenagers. We showcase examples of successful prevention programs in schools and communities, emphasizing the importance of early intervention.

Teenage Depression Example: Let's consider a 16-year-old named Alex. As a high school student, Alex faces intense academic pressure and struggles to fit in with peers. He often withdraws from social activities and has difficulty sleeping. His parents, noticing these changes in behaviour, decide to have an open conversation with him about his feelings. This open dialogue leads to early intervention. Alex's school also implements a mental health awareness program that helps teenagers like him better manage stress and seek help when needed, contributing to their emotional well-being.

Prevention and Intervention in Teenage Depression: In a community, a high school partners with local mental health organizations to create a preventive program for teenage depression. This program includes stress management workshops, peer support groups, and regular mental health check-ins. Over the years, they notice a significant decrease in the prevalence of depression among their students.

This example illustrates how proactive prevention strategies, early intervention, and community collaboration can make a substantial difference in the mental health of teenagers.

Preventing and intervening in teenage depression are proactive steps that can set the course for a lifetime of well-being.

1. **School-Based Programs:** The "Wellbeing in Post-Primary Schools" program aims to support the mental health and well-being of students in Irish secondary schools by providing guidance and resources to schools and teachers. It encourages the inclusion of well-being and mental health education in the school curriculum and promotes a whole-school approach to well-being.

2. **Community Workshops:** Jigsaw is a national youth mental health program that provides a range of services and support to young people between the ages of 12 and 25. It includes community workshops, educational resources, and support for young people, parents, and teachers.

3. **Online Support Groups:** SpunOut.ie is a youth-led organization that offers a website and online platform where young people can find information, resources, and a supportive community to discuss mental health, well-being, and various other issues.

The platform includes articles, blogs, videos, and forums where teenagers can share their experiences, ask questions, and connect with peers who understand their struggles.

These examples emphasize the significant role that proactive prevention programs in schools and communities, early intervention by professionals, and peer support can play in addressing teenage depression. They showcase how timely support can make a significant difference in the lives of teenagers facing mental health challenges.

Depression in the Elderly: Navigating the Golden Years

Late-Life Depression

Depression in the elderly, often referred to as late-life depression, has its own distinct features. We examine how life transitions, medical comorbidities, and social isolation can contribute to this condition.

Eleanor's Story: The Weight of Loss

Eleanor, at 78, had always been a resilient and independent woman. She had faced life's challenges with a determined spirit. However, after the loss of her husband, whom she had been married to for over 50 years, she found herself trapped in a cycle of grief and despair.

Eleanor's late-life depression was marked by profound loneliness and a sense of emptiness. She described it as if a piece of her heart was missing, and she struggled to find joy in the activities she once loved.

Seeking professional help was the turning point for Eleanor. With the guidance of a therapist, she was able to confront her grief, process her emotions, and slowly find her way back to a life with meaning.

John's Journey: Isolation and the Silent Struggle

John, at 82, had always been known as the jovial grandfather of the family. However, in his late 70s, he found himself feeling increasingly isolated. The passing of many friends and family members, coupled with physical health issues, led to a growing sense of despair.

John's late-life depression was marked by a profound sense of isolation. He felt disconnected from his loved ones, unable to engage in the social activities he once enjoyed. His journey to recovery began with the support of a home healthcare worker who recognized the signs of depression. Together, they created a plan to reintegrate John into social activities, fostering a sense of belonging and connection that had long been absent from his life.

Maggie's Experience: The Struggle to Seek Help

Maggie, at 85, had always been a strong and self-reliant woman. For years, she had been the caregiver for her husband, who had Alzheimer's disease. When he passed away, she believed it was her duty to grieve silently and not burden her family with her pain.

Maggie's late-life depression was marked by a deep sense of guilt and isolation. She felt trapped in a cycle of sadness but struggled to admit her suffering. It was her daughter, who recognized the signs, who gently encouraged her to seek professional help. Therapy provided Maggie with a safe space to share her grief and understand that seeking help was not a sign of weakness, but an act of self-compassion.

These examples of elderly individuals experiencing late-life depression highlight the unique challenges they face, including grief, isolation, and a reluctance to seek help. Through support, whether from professionals or loved ones, they were able to find their way towards recovery, demonstrating that it's never too late to address and overcome late-life depression.

Distinguishing from Normal Aging

Distinguishing depression from normal aging can be challenging. In this section, we explored how the symptoms of depression, such as persistent sadness, fatigue, and cognitive impairments, can be differentiated from the natural aging process. Examples of both older adults and parent's perspectives on recognizing depression in the elderly. We provide guidance on how to approach this sensitive topic and initiate conversations about mental health with older family members.

A Holistic Perspective

Depression affects individuals of all ages, and understanding its manifestations in different age groups is crucial. This chapter illustrated the need for age-specific approaches to diagnosis, treatment, and support. By recognizing the unique challenges and considerations of childhood, teenage, and late-life depression, we set the stage for a more comprehensive and empathetic approach to addressing depression across the lifespan. The journey to understanding and overcoming depression extends from the earliest years to the golden ones, encompassing the full spectrum of human experience.

Chapter 12: Depression and Other Conditions

Depression is a multifaceted condition that often intersects with various other mental health and medical conditions. This chapter looks into the intricate relationship between depression and comorbid conditions, including anxiety disorders, substance abuse, and chronic illness. Understanding these complex interplays is pivotal for effective intervention and support.

Anxiety Disorders: The Overlapping Emotions

Understanding the Comorbidity

Comorbidity between depression and anxiety disorders is common and can significantly impact an individual's well-being. This section provides a comprehensive overview of this co-occurrence and the intricate ways in which symptoms overlap.

Examples of comorbid depression and anxiety:

Anna's Struggle: The Dual Weight of Darkness

Anna, in her mid-30s, has lived with comorbid depression and anxiety for most of her adult life. She describes her experience as a relentless tug-of-war between overwhelming sadness and paralyzing fear. At times, she feels trapped in her own mind, unable to escape the thoughts that tell her she's not good enough.

One of the most challenging aspects of her experience is the constant battle to find a balance. On some days, depression pulls her into a deep sense of hopelessness, while on others, anxiety propels her into panic and self-doubt.

For Anna, the key to managing comorbid depression and anxiety has been finding a supportive therapist who can help her untangle these complex emotions and develop practical coping strategies.

David's Daily Struggle: The Fear of the Unknown

David, in his early 40s, has been living with comorbid depression and anxiety for as long as he can remember. He describes it as a perpetual state of uncertainty. Every decision, from what to have for breakfast to major life choices, is accompanied by a nagging sense of dread. His mind races with "what ifs" and "worst-case scenarios."

For David, the challenge lies in the interplay between his depression and anxiety. Depression often saps his motivation and makes him feel that there's no point in trying. Anxiety, on the other hand, fills him with worry about the consequences of not taking action. To manage this delicate balance, he relies on medication, regular therapy sessions, and a strong support network of friends and family.

Olivia's Journey: The Pursuit of Peace

Olivia, in her late 20s, has found herself grappling with comorbid depression and anxiety in the competitive world of academia. She describes it as a daily marathon, where her emotions vacillate between a crushing sense of despair and a frantic urgency to prove herself.

One of the most significant challenges for Olivia has been the stigma surrounding mental health in her academic environment.

She feared judgment from her peers and mentors, which initially prevented her from seeking help. Eventually, she found solace in a university counselling centre and connected with a supportive group of peers who understood her experience. Olivia's journey highlights the importance of seeking help and challenging the stigma associated with mental health issues.

These examples shed light on the complexities of living with comorbid depression and anxiety. They illustrate the constant struggle to find equilibrium between two powerful emotional states. Through therapy, medication, and the support of loved ones, these individuals have discovered ways to navigate the challenges and find moments of peace and hope in their lives.

The Shared Features

Depression and anxiety disorders share common features, including excessive worry, irritability, and sleep disturbances.

Comorbid depression and anxiety often coexist, and it's crucial to recognize that they can manifest differently in each individual. Tailored treatment plans are essential. Cognitive-behavioural therapy (CBT) has been a successful approach for many. It allows patients to address negative thought patterns, which are common in both conditions. Medication may also be considered, and its selection depends on the predominant symptoms. Regular check-ins with a therapist are vital to track progress.

While depression and anxiety can share symptoms, understanding their unique presentations is key. Depression is often marked by pervasive sadness, loss of interest, and low energy, while anxiety is characterized by excessive worry, restlessness, and heightened arousal. Medication can help alleviate these symptoms. Antidepressants may work well for comorbid conditions, but they should be prescribed carefully.

Integrating lifestyle changes is instrumental in managing comorbid depression and anxiety. Regular exercise, a balanced diet, and sufficient sleep can significantly impact both conditions. Additionally, mindfulness practices and relaxation techniques are essential for grounding and managing anxious thoughts. A strong support network, including friends, family, and support groups, plays a critical role in the recovery process.

Comorbid conditions often feed off each other, creating a vicious cycle. It's vital to explore the root causes and triggers of both depression and anxiety.

Self-awareness is a powerful tool, and I encourage my clients to journal and track their emotions. This process can reveal patterns and help individuals anticipate and manage their symptoms. Therapy provides a safe space for exploring these emotions and developing coping strategies.

It's essential to address both depression and anxiety simultaneously. These conditions are closely intertwined, and treating one without considering the other may not yield the best results.

Setting achievable goals, challenging negative thought patterns, and gradually exposing individuals to situations that trigger anxiety. This desensitization process, alongside support from loved ones, can lead to improved well-being.

The significance of personalized treatment plans that consider the unique needs and experiences of individuals with comorbid depression and anxiety. Comprehensive care, including therapy, medication, lifestyle adjustments, and a strong support system, is crucial for managing these challenging conditions effectively.

Integrated Treatment

Addressing comorbid depression and anxiety often necessitates an integrated approach. In this section, we explore various integrated treatment modalities, such as cognitive-behavioural therapy for comorbidity (CBT-C), dialectical behaviour therapy (DBT), and exposure therapy.

Example: Sarah's Journey with Comorbid Depression and Anxiety

Sarah, a 34-year-old marketing manager, has been struggling with comorbid depression and anxiety. She has been feeling persistently sad, unmotivated, and overwhelmed by constant worry and nervousness. Her sleep patterns have been disrupted, and she often finds herself unable to concentrate at work.

Assessment and Formulation: Sarah's therapist begins by conducting a thorough assessment to understand the extent of her depression and anxiety and their unique features. Sarah's therapist finds that her depression symptoms include low mood, fatigue, and a loss of interest in activities she once enjoyed. Her anxiety symptoms encompass excessive worry, restlessness, and physical symptoms like muscle tension and heart palpitations. A comprehensive assessment allows for a tailored treatment plan.

Setting Treatment Goals: Together, Sarah and her therapist establish clear treatment goals. These may include reducing the frequency and intensity of depressive episodes, learning to manage anxiety-related thoughts and physical symptoms, and improving overall well-being and quality of life.

Cognitive Restructuring: Sarah's therapist uses cognitive restructuring to address her negative thought patterns associated with both conditions.

Sarah has a tendency to catastrophize situations, believing the worst will happen, which fuels her anxiety. She also holds a strong inner critic, leading to self-deprecating thoughts that exacerbate her depression. Through CBT, Sarah learns to identify these thought patterns, challenge their validity, and replace them with more balanced and rational alternatives.

Behavioural Activation: Sarah's therapist introduces behavioural activation to help her combat depression. Sarah and her therapist work together to identify activities that once brought her joy but have been abandoned due to her low mood.

They create a gradual schedule of pleasurable and fulfilling activities, which helps Sarah regain a sense of accomplishment and happiness.

Exposure and Relaxation Techniques: To address Sarah's anxiety, her therapist employs exposure therapy, gradually exposing her to situations that trigger her anxiety. Simultaneously, relaxation techniques like deep breathing and progressive muscle relaxation are taught to help her manage the physical symptoms of anxiety.

Homework and Self-Monitoring: Sarah is given homework assignments to practice the skills she learns in therapy. This may include keeping a thought journal to monitor negative thinking patterns or conducting relaxation exercises daily. The therapist reviews Sarah's progress during sessions.

Support System: Sarah's therapist encourages her to maintain a strong support system of friends and family. Building a support network is integral to her recovery, as it provides emotional support and encourages her to engage in social activities.

Review and Adjustments: Throughout the therapy process, Sarah and her therapist regularly review her progress and adjust the treatment plan as needed. The therapy continues until Sarah feels equipped to manage her depression and anxiety effectively.

Over the course of therapy, Sarah learns to differentiate between her depressive and anxious thoughts and develop coping strategies for both conditions.

She experiences fewer depressive episodes and manages her anxiety more effectively, ultimately improving her overall well-being.

This example illustrates how CBT-C can be tailored to address the unique challenges of individuals with comorbid depression and anxiety, helping them develop coping strategies and improve their mental health.

Example: Emily's Journey with Specific Phobias and Emotional Dysregulation

Emily, a 28-year-old woman, has been struggling with specific phobias, particularly a fear of flying, and emotional dysregulation.

She experiences intense anxiety and panic attacks when faced with the prospect of air travel, which has restricted her personal and professional life. She also struggles with emotional outbursts, difficulty managing distress, and a history of self-harming behaviours.

Assessment and Formulation: Emily's therapist conducts a thorough assessment to understand the nature of her phobias and emotional dysregulation. It is revealed that Emily's fear of flying is linked to traumatic experiences during a previous flight. Her emotional dysregulation is a result of her inability to effectively manage distress, leading to impulsive behaviours. The therapist identifies that Emily's emotional instability often exacerbates her phobia.

Setting Treatment Goals: Together, Emily and her therapist establish clear treatment goals, including reducing her fear of flying, developing distress tolerance skills, and improving her emotional regulation to reduce self-harming behaviours.

Dialectical Behaviour Therapy (DBT): Emily's therapist introduces DBT, a structured and evidence-based approach that combines cognitive-behavioural techniques with mindfulness. Emily learns emotion regulation skills to better understand and manage her emotional responses. She practices mindfulness meditation to stay present and cope with distress without acting impulsively. Through DBT, Emily builds interpersonal effectiveness, improving her ability to communicate her needs and boundaries.

Exposure Therapy: To address her specific phobias, Emily's therapist implements exposure therapy. They start with gradual exposure to the fear of flying. Initially, Emily might simply look at pictures of airplanes or watch videos about air travel. Over time, she progresses to more challenging exposure tasks, such as visiting an airport without boarding a plane. With each step, she practices relaxation techniques and mindfulness to manage anxiety and distress effectively.

Homework and Self-Monitoring: Emily is given homework assignments to practice the skills she learns in therapy. For example, she keeps a diary to track her emotional responses and uses distress tolerance techniques when she feels overwhelmed. She also records her progress in facing her fear of flying.

Support System: Emily's therapist encourages her to maintain a support system of friends and family who can provide emotional support during her journey. They educate her loved ones about her therapy process to ensure they can be supportive.

Review and Adjustments: Throughout the therapy process, Emily and her therapist regularly review her progress and adjust the treatment plan as needed. The therapy continues until Emily feels confident in her ability to manage her emotional dysregulation and her fear of flying effectively.

By combining DBT with exposure therapy, Emily learns to manage her emotional dysregulation, allowing her to approach exposure to her specific phobia with increased emotional stability. As a result, she can gradually confront her fear of flying and regain control over her life. This combined approach empowers her to face her phobia with greater emotional resilience.

Substance Abuse: The Vicious Cycle

The Bidirectional Relationship

Depression and substance abuse often co-occur, creating a complex bidirectional relationship. We examine how individuals may turn to substances as a coping mechanism for depressive symptoms and how substance abuse can, in turn, contribute to the onset of depression.

Example: Daniel's Struggle with Depression and Substance Abuse

Daniel, a 30-year-old office worker, had experienced depressive symptoms since his late teens. He often felt overwhelmed by feelings of sadness, hopelessness, and social isolation. He had difficulty finding joy in activities he once enjoyed and struggled with maintaining relationships.

Depression as the Precursor: Daniel's depression was the initial challenge he faced. It was a constant companion, affecting his personal and professional life. He found it challenging to concentrate at work and often withdrew from social interactions. His depressive symptoms left him feeling emotionally drained and desperate for relief.

Turning to Substances as a Coping Mechanism: In an attempt to alleviate the emotional pain and emptiness associated with depression, Daniel turned to alcohol as a coping mechanism. Initially, he found that alcohol provided temporary relief from his depressive symptoms. It numbed his feelings of sadness and anxiety and allowed him to temporarily escape from the weight of his emotional struggles.

Substance Abuse as a Contributing Factor: However, over time, Daniel's alcohol use escalated, and he began to rely on it as a way to self-medicate his depression. This substance abuse further complicated his mental health. The depressive symptoms intensified, and he experienced a downward spiral where alcohol became both a coping mechanism and a source of distress.

His physical and mental health deteriorated, leading to a significant disruption in his life.

The Bidirectional Relationship: In Daniel's case, the relationship between depression and substance abuse became bidirectional. Depression was the initial trigger for his substance abuse, as he sought relief from emotional pain. However, substance abuse, in turn, contributed to the worsening of his depression. This bidirectional cycle made it increasingly difficult for him to break free from the grip of both conditions.

Treatment and Recovery: Daniel eventually sought professional help, acknowledging the destructive nature of this bidirectional relationship. He entered a dual diagnosis treatment program, which addressed both his depression and substance abuse simultaneously. Through therapy, he learned healthier coping mechanisms for managing his depressive symptoms and was provided with strategies to overcome his addiction.

This Example demonstrates the complexity of the bidirectional relationship between depression and substance abuse. For many individuals, substances initially serve as a means of self-medication for depressive symptoms, but the continued use of substances can contribute to the exacerbation of depression, creating a challenging cycle that requires specialized treatment and support for recovery. In Daniel's case, recognizing this bidirectional relationship and seeking help was the first step toward a path to healing and recovery.

Breaking the Cycle

Breaking the cycle of depression and substance abuse is possible, but it requires a multifaceted approach. This section looks into the principles of dual diagnosis treatment, discussing evidence-based approaches.

The principles of dual diagnosis treatment, which addresses both mental health and substance use disorders, are multifaceted and require a comprehensive and integrated approach.

Here, we discuss some key principles and evidence-based approaches such as Motivational Enhancement Therapy (MET) and Contingency Management:

1. Integrated Assessment and Treatment:

- Individuals with dual diagnoses should receive integrated assessment and treatment that addresses both their mental health and substance use issues simultaneously. This approach recognizes the interplay between these conditions and the need to treat them as interconnected.

2. Motivational Enhancement Therapy (MET):

- MET is an evidence-based approach designed to enhance an individual's motivation to change their behaviour, particularly concerning substance use. It is a client-centred approach where therapists work with clients to explore their ambivalence about change and help them identify their own reasons for seeking treatment. MET is based on principles of empathy, support, and collaborative goal setting.

3. Contingency Management:

- Contingency Management is another evidence-based approach that utilizes a system of rewards and incentives to encourage abstinence from substances. It reinforces positive behaviours, such as staying drug-free, through tangible rewards. This approach helps individuals build new, healthier habits and behaviours.

4. Medication-Assisted Treatment (MAT):

- MAT involves the use of medications in conjunction with counselling and therapy to treat substance use disorders. For individuals with dual diagnoses, MAT can be particularly effective, as it addresses the physiological aspects of addiction while also addressing mental health concerns.

5. Cognitive-Behavioural Therapy (CBT):

- CBT helps individuals identify and change negative thought patterns and behaviours associated with both mental health and substance use disorders. It provides practical strategies for managing triggers and developing healthier coping mechanisms.

6. Trauma-Informed Care:

- Many individuals with dual diagnoses have a history of trauma, which can contribute to both their mental health and substance use issues. Trauma-informed care recognizes the impact of trauma on an individual's well-being and provides a safe and supportive environment for healing.

7. Supportive and Holistic Approach:

- Treatment should be holistic, addressing not only the mental health and substance use aspects but also other life areas, such as housing, employment, and relationships. A supportive and non-judgmental approach is crucial to building trust and promoting recovery.

8. Relapse Prevention:

- Relapse prevention strategies are a critical component of dual diagnosis treatment. These help individuals identify triggers and high-risk situations and develop coping strategies to prevent relapse.

9. Long-Term Care and Follow-Up:

- Dual diagnosis treatment often requires ongoing care and support, as recovery can be a lengthy process. Follow-up and aftercare services are essential to help individuals maintain their progress.

10. Recovery-Oriented Approach:

- The ultimate goal of dual diagnosis treatment is not only symptom management but also helping individuals achieve a meaningful and fulfilling life in recovery. The recovery-oriented approach focuses on improving overall well-being.

These principles, along with evidence-based approaches like MET and Contingency Management, provide a framework for effective dual diagnosis treatment.

It's important to tailor treatment to each individual's unique needs, considering the specific mental health and substance use challenges they face.

Support and Relapse Prevention

Maintaining recovery from comorbid depression and substance abuse is an ongoing process that involves support and relapse prevention strategies. We explore the role of therapy, 12-step programs, harm reduction, and peer support in fostering lasting recovery.

1. The Role of Therapy:

Example - John's Journey to Recovery: John, a 42-year-old man, had been struggling with comorbid depression and alcohol addiction for many years. He started individual therapy with a licensed therapist who specialized in dual diagnosis. Through therapy, John addressed the underlying emotional pain contributing to his depression and alcohol use. He learned healthy coping mechanisms, developed self-awareness, and worked on rebuilding his self-esteem. The therapist also helped him create a relapse prevention plan and encouraged him to continue therapy to maintain his recovery. John found that therapy was a safe and supportive space for him to explore his emotions and build the skills needed for lasting recovery.

2. The Role of 12-Step Programs:

Example - Sarah's Sobriety Through a 12-Step Program: Sarah, a 35-year-old woman, had been battling comorbid depression and a prescription drug addiction.

She decided to attend a 12-step program, such as Alcoholics Anonymous (AA) or Narcotics Anonymous (NA).

The 12-step program provided her with a structured framework for addressing her addiction and connecting with peers who understood her struggles. Sarah found a sponsor within the program, a mentor who guided her through the steps and provided support when cravings or depressive episodes occurred. The principles of honesty, accountability, and fellowship in the 12-step program played a crucial role in Sarah's recovery journey.

3. The Role of Harm Reduction:

Example - David's Journey with Opioid Dependence and Depression: David, a 28-year-old, had been using opioids to self-medicate his depression. He started a harm reduction program that focused on minimizing the harm associated with drug use while working towards abstinence. David received education on safer use, access to clean needles, and information on overdose prevention. Over time, he was gradually able to reduce his opioid use and, with the help of therapy, address his depression. Harm reduction allowed David to take gradual steps towards recovery while minimizing the associated risks.

4. The Role of Peer Support:

Example - Emily's Supportive Peer Network: Emily, a 30-year-old, had struggled with comorbid depression and alcohol addiction for years. She joined a peer support group for individuals with dual diagnoses. In this group, she found understanding and non-judgmental peers who had faced similar challenges.

They shared their experiences, coping strategies, and provided encouragement during difficult times. The peer support network gave Emily a sense of belonging and connection, which played a vital role in her ongoing recovery.

These examples highlight the significance of therapy, 12-step programs, harm reduction, and peer support in fostering lasting recovery for individuals with comorbid depression and substance abuse. Each approach provides a unique set of tools and resources to help individuals manage their conditions and work towards a healthier, more fulfilling life in recovery.

Chronic Illness: The Dual Burden

Depression as a Comorbidity

Depression frequently accompanies chronic illnesses, adding an extra layer of complexity to the individual's health journey. We examine how the burden of chronic illness can contribute to depressive symptoms.

Case Study: Maria's Struggle with Chronic Illness and Depression

Maria, a 45-year-old woman, had been living with multiple sclerosis (MS) for over a decade. MS is a chronic and progressive autoimmune disease that affects the central nervous system. As a result of her condition, Maria faced a range of physical and emotional challenges.

Physical Limitations and Independence: Due to the progression of her MS, Maria experienced increasing physical limitations. Simple daily tasks, like getting out of bed, preparing meals, and walking, became increasingly difficult. She was no longer able to work, leading to a loss of financial independence. These physical limitations made her feel reliant on others, which was a significant blow to her self-esteem.

Pain and Discomfort: The chronic pain and discomfort associated with MS became a constant presence in Maria's life. Nerve pain, muscle spasms, and fatigue were her daily companions. The ongoing physical suffering added to her emotional distress and drained her energy, leaving her feeling overwhelmed.

Isolation and Limited Social Activities: Maria's symptoms often left her too fatigued to engage in social activities. She withdrew from friends and family gatherings, leading to feelings of isolation. Her world became increasingly small, and she felt disconnected from her support network.

Financial and Healthcare Stress: The cost of her medical treatments and specialized care placed a significant financial burden on Maria and her family. She struggled to navigate the complexities of insurance, healthcare bills, and disability benefits. The constant financial stress added to her worries and further contributed to her depressive symptoms.

Loss of Future Plans: Maria had to let go of many of her future plans and dreams due to her chronic illness. She could no longer pursue a career, travel, or engage in physical activities she once loved. This loss of future possibilities created a sense of hopelessness and despair.

Depressive Symptoms: Over time, Maria began to experience a range of depressive symptoms, including persistent sadness, feelings of worthlessness, difficulty concentrating, and a loss of interest in activities she once enjoyed. Her physical symptoms and the impact of her chronic illness had contributed to the development of depression.

The Complex Relationship: Maria's case illustrates the complex relationship between chronic illness and depression. The physical limitations, pain, isolation, financial stress, and loss of future plans associated with her chronic illness all played a role in the development of depressive symptoms. These emotional struggles added an extra layer of complexity to her health journey.

Treatment and Support: Maria sought help from a mental health professional who specialized in treating individuals with chronic illnesses. She participated in therapy to address her depressive symptoms and develop coping strategies for managing the emotional impact of her illness. Additionally, she joined support groups for individuals with MS, which provided her with a sense of community and understanding.

This example emphasizes the importance of recognizing and addressing the emotional challenges that often accompany chronic illnesses. It demonstrates the need for a comprehensive approach that considers both the physical and emotional aspects of an individual's health journey.

Managing the Dual Burden

Managing comorbid depression and chronic illness requires a holistic approach. This section explores various interventions, including psychoeducation, self-management strategies, and medication.

Example: James' Journey to Managing Comorbid Depression and Diabetes

James, a 50-year-old man, had been living with type 2 diabetes for over a decade. His chronic illness required daily blood glucose monitoring, medication, and dietary restrictions. However, he also experienced comorbid depression, which added an extra layer of complexity to his health management.

Psychoeducation: James's healthcare team provided him with psychoeducation about the relationship between diabetes and depression. He learned that there's a bidirectional relationship, meaning that uncontrolled diabetes can contribute to depressive symptoms, and depression can make it harder to manage diabetes effectively. Understanding this connection helped James recognize that addressing his mental health was crucial for his overall well-being.

Self-Management Strategies: With the guidance of a healthcare professional, James developed self-management strategies. He learned techniques to monitor and regulate his blood glucose levels effectively. These strategies included regular exercise, a balanced diet, and taking his diabetes medication as prescribed. Additionally, he acquired skills for recognizing the signs of depressive episodes and strategies to cope with them.

Medication Management: James's healthcare team prescribed both diabetes medication and antidepressants to manage his conditions. They carefully monitored his medication regimen to ensure there were no adverse interactions between the two types of medication. James also received guidance on potential side effects and how to manage them.

Lifestyle Modifications: James made lifestyle modifications to accommodate both his diabetes and depression. He incorporated stress-reduction techniques like mindfulness meditation into his daily routine to manage depressive symptoms. He also joined a diabetes support group, which provided emotional support, and he attended therapy sessions to address his depression.

Regular Check-Ins: James maintained regular check-ins with his healthcare team. This included visits to his primary care physician, endocrinologist for diabetes management, and a mental health professional for his depression. These healthcare providers worked together to ensure a cohesive treatment plan that addressed both his chronic illness and depression.

Support Network: James actively engaged his support network, including his family, friends, and the diabetes support group. They provided emotional support and accountability. By discussing his challenges and achievements with others who understood his situation, James felt less isolated.

Long-Term Management: Over time, James continued to manage his comorbid conditions effectively. He recognized that it was an ongoing journey and that he needed to prioritize self-care and mental health to maintain his well-being.

James's case exemplifies how a holistic approach, which includes psychoeducation, self-management strategies, medication management, lifestyle modifications, regular check-ins, and a strong support network, can be applied to manage comorbid depression and chronic illness. This approach recognizes the interplay between physical and mental health and emphasizes the importance of addressing both aspects for a healthier and more fulfilling life.

The Role of Social Support

Social support plays a pivotal role in managing depression in the context of chronic illness. The significance of family, friends cannot be underestimated.

Example: Sarah's Journey to Managing Depression and Rheumatoid Arthritis

Sarah, a 38-year-old woman, had been living with rheumatoid arthritis (RA) for several years. RA is an autoimmune disease that causes chronic pain and inflammation in the joints. Over time, the pain and physical limitations took a toll on her mental health, and she developed depression.

The Role of Family and Friends: Sarah's family and friends played a pivotal role in her journey to manage depression alongside her chronic illness. Her husband, John, was her primary caregiver and source of emotional support. He attended medical appointments with her, helped with daily tasks during flare-ups, and provided reassurance during moments of despair.

Understanding and Empathy: Sarah's close friends were understanding and empathetic. They made an effort to educate themselves about RA and depression, which allowed them to provide better emotional support. When Sarah couldn't participate in activities due to her illness, her friends organized gatherings that accommodated her limitations. This understanding and flexibility helped reduce feelings of isolation.

Emotional Encouragement: Sarah's family and friends consistently provided emotional encouragement. They reminded her of her strength and resilience during challenging times. This emotional reinforcement served as a motivational factor and a reminder that she wasn't alone in her struggle.

Active Involvement: Sarah's support network actively involved themselves in her self-care. They encouraged her to attend therapy, reminding her that it was a sign of strength to seek professional help. They also participated in physical activities suitable for her condition, such as gentle yoga or walks, which further contributed to her well-being.

Providing a Safe Space: Sarah's family and friends created a safe space for open communication. They actively listened when she wanted to talk about her challenges, pain, and emotional struggles. This open dialogue allowed Sarah to express her feelings, reducing the emotional burden she carried.

Reducing Stigma: By openly discussing her depression and RA, Sarah's family and friends helped reduce the stigma associated with mental health issues. This open and accepting environment made it easier for Sarah to seek treatment and share her experiences with her support network.

The Result: Sarah's journey to managing depression and RA was challenging, but her strong support network played a pivotal role in her recovery. With the help of therapy, medication, and the unwavering support of her family and friends, she was able to better manage her depression. Their understanding, empathy, and active involvement helped her maintain her mental health while dealing with a chronic illness.

This example demonstrates that the significance of family and friends cannot be underestimated when managing depression within the context of chronic illness. Their understanding, support, and willingness to actively participate in an individual's care can make a substantial difference in their ability to cope with the emotional challenges associated with chronic illness

A Holistic Perspective

Depression rarely exists in isolation, and its intersection with other conditions presents unique challenges. This chapter illustrates the need for a comprehensive and empathetic approach to addressing comorbid conditions. By recognizing the complex relationship between depression and anxiety disorders, substance abuse, and chronic illness, we set the foundation for a more integrated approach to mental and physical health. The journey to understanding and overcoming depression extends beyond its own borders, encompassing the full spectrum of human experience and challenges.

Chapter 13: Living with Depression

Example 1: John's Journey: Finding Light in the Darkness

Background: John is a 35-year-old individual who has been struggling with depression for several years. He works as a marketing manager at a mid-sized company. Despite his professional success, he has been facing a persistent sense of sadness, self-doubt, and withdrawal from social activities. His friends and family have noticed his changing behaviour, and he has started missing work due to his emotional state.

Turning Point: One evening, after a particularly difficult day at work, John had a moment of clarity. He realized that he couldn't continue living with this overwhelming sadness and needed help. He reached out to a close friend and shared his struggles, which led to a heartfelt conversation about seeking professional assistance.

Path to Recovery: John started therapy with a licensed psychologist who specializes in treating depression. He also consulted a psychiatrist who prescribed antidepressant medication. In therapy, John explored the roots of his depression, including past traumatic experiences and negative thought patterns. Over time, he learned coping strategies and gradually regained a sense of self-worth. He experienced setbacks along the way but was determined to keep moving forward.

Role of Support: John's journey to recovery was significantly aided by the unwavering support of his close friends and family. They offered emotional assistance, attended therapy sessions with him when needed, and encouraged open conversations about his mental health. This support network played a crucial role in his healing process.

Example 2: Sarah's Story: The Strength of Resilience

Background: Sarah, a 40-year-old woman, has faced numerous challenges throughout her life. She experienced childhood trauma and grew up in a tumultuous family environment. These early experiences contributed to her struggle with depression, which intensified as she reached adulthood. Sarah works as a social worker and has always been dedicated to helping others, but she found it challenging to extend the same compassion to herself.

Navigating Mental Health Services: After years of emotional turmoil, Sarah decided to seek help. She began therapy with a clinical psychologist who specialized in trauma and depression. It was a challenging process as she had to confront painful memories and emotions from her past. She also started taking antidepressant medication as recommended by her psychiatrist.

Finding Resilience: The core of Sarah's story is her remarkable resilience. Through therapy, she learned to recognize and challenge negative thought patterns that had haunted her for years.

She also developed self-compassion and gradually began to rebuild her self-esteem. These personal growth milestones were essential to her journey to recovery.

Offering Hope to Others: Sarah's transformative journey led her to engage in advocacy work. She started volunteering at a local mental health support organization and began sharing her story to offer hope and support to others facing similar challenges. Her experiences with trauma, depression, and recovery allowed her to connect with individuals who needed understanding and empathy.

Example 3: Michael's Resilience: A Journey of Rediscovery

Background: Michael, a 28-year-old artist and musician, found himself immersed in a deep depression. He felt disconnected from his passions and interests, which included creating art and playing music. He withdrew from his social circle and found it increasingly difficult to experience joy in life.

A Therapeutic Journey: Michael embarked on a therapeutic journey to reclaim his love for art and music. He started attending psychotherapy with an art therapist who specialized in creative expression as a form of healing. Through art therapy, he began to reconnect with his emotions and rekindle his creative spirit.

Rediscovering Joy: As Michael engaged in art therapy, he gradually started to experience moments of joy and fulfilment. Creating art became a therapeutic outlet for his emotions, allowing him to express his inner struggles and find solace.

He also joined a local music group and reignited his passion for playing music, which brought a sense of purpose back into his life.

A Message of Resilience: Michael's story offers a message of resilience and rediscovery. He emphasizes the importance of seeking professional help and not losing hope, even when the future seems bleak. Through the therapeutic journey, he discovered that healing and joy could be found in the very passions that depression had taken away from him.

Insights and Coping Mechanisms

Through these personal stories, several common insights and coping mechanisms emerge:

- **The Power of Professional Help:** All of these individuals sought the assistance of mental health professionals. Therapy and, in some cases, medication, were pivotal in managing their symptoms.

- **Support Systems:** Family and friends played a critical role in their lives. They provided a safety net, encouragement, and understanding.

- **Self-Care Rituals:** Coping mechanisms often included daily self-care rituals. Regular exercise, meditation, journaling, and a balanced diet were essential elements.

- **Resilience and Acceptance:** These warriors embraced the idea that resilience is not the absence of struggle but the strength to deal with it. Acceptance of their conditions was a significant turning point.

Embracing the Journey

The stories of Sarah, Micheal and John are living testaments to the potential for growth, healing, and happiness despite the enduring presence of depression. They remind us that the path to well-being is not always linear, and setbacks are part of the journey.

While depression might not completely vanish, it can be managed, and life can still be deeply fulfilling. These individuals are not merely surviving; they are thriving. Their stories inspire us to embrace our journeys, understand the value of resilience, and seek help when needed.

Depression does not define their lives. They have rewritten their narratives, and you can, too. By acknowledging the challenges and embracing the support systems and strategies that work for you, you can find joy, purpose, and a fulfilling life even in the face of depression.

Understanding Depression

Understanding depression is the foundation of effective support. To truly grasp what your loved one is going through, you need to educate yourself about depression. Learn about the various forms it can take and the common signs and symptoms.

Depression is often misunderstood as merely feeling sad, but it can manifest in more subtle ways, such as changes in sleep patterns, appetite, and the loss of interest in activities that were once enjoyed. Understanding these aspects of depression allows you to approach the situation with empathy and knowledge. It's essential to acknowledge that depression is a complex mental health condition that can affect anyone, and your knowledge can help reduce the stigma surrounding it.

Open Communication

The first step in supporting a loved one is establishing open and empathetic communication. Begin the conversation by expressing your genuine concern and care for their well-being. Let them know that you're there to listen and offer support. When they share their thoughts and feelings, practice active listening. This means being fully present in the moment, giving them your full attention, and avoiding distractions. It's crucial to listen without judgment, allowing them to express themselves freely. Create a safe space where they feel comfortable sharing their experiences, fears, and challenges. By listening actively and without judgment, you can make them feel heard and understood, which is essential in the recovery process.

Seeking Professional Help

While offering emotional support is valuable, it's vital to recognize your limitations. Depression often requires professional intervention. Once you've established open communication, encourage your loved one to seek professional help.

Approach this topic with sensitivity, emphasizing that consulting a mental health professional, such as a therapist or psychiatrist, is a positive and courageous step toward healing. Provide guidance on how to find a suitable professional, assist in scheduling appointments, and offer to accompany them if it makes them feel more comfortable. Your support during this process can make a significant difference in their willingness to seek treatment. Remember that professional help can provide the tools and strategies necessary to manage and recover from depression effectively.

Active Listening

Active listening is a fundamental aspect of providing emotional support. When your loved one shares their thoughts and feelings, practice active listening. This means not only hearing their words but also understanding the emotions behind them. Give them your full attention, maintain eye contact, and avoid interrupting or offering solutions unless they ask for advice. Allow them to express themselves freely and openly. Your active listening communicates that you genuinely care about their emotions and experiences, which can provide comfort and reassurance during their difficult moments.

Empathy and Validation

Empathy and validation are powerful tools for emotional support. Try to understand your loved one's emotions from their perspective. Put yourself in their shoes and acknowledge their feelings. Show empathy by expressing understanding and compassion.

Validation means confirming that their emotions are valid and acceptable. Let them know that it's okay to feel the way they do and that you're there to support them unconditionally. Your empathetic responses and validation create a sense of trust and connection, making them feel heard, valued, and less alone in their struggle.

Patience and Understanding

Recovery from depression is not a linear journey. It can involve ups and downs, setbacks, and gradual progress. Patience is essential in supporting someone with depression. Understand that improvement may be slow or non-linear, and don't express frustration or impatience. Your continued understanding and support during these challenging times can be a source of strength for your loved one. Reiterate your commitment to being there for them throughout their journey, no matter how long it takes. Your unwavering patience and understanding can help alleviate some of the emotional burden they carry.

Practical Support

Practical support involves helping your loved one with daily tasks that they may find challenging during depressive episodes. Offer assistance with chores, cooking, cleaning, or running errands when they struggle to manage these responsibilities. Recognize that depression can make even the simplest tasks feel overwhelming. By offering practical help, you can alleviate some of their burdens and provide relief. Your support in managing daily life can help them conserve their energy and focus on their emotional well-being.

Encouraging Self-Care

Encouraging self-care is pivotal for someone with depression. Depression can often lead to neglect of self-care routines, such as a balanced diet, regular exercise, and a consistent sleep schedule. Offer your support in maintaining these routines. Cook healthy meals together, engage in physical activities like walks or yoga, and help create a soothing bedtime routine. Encourage them to prioritize their physical and mental well-being. Self-care practices can significantly impact their mental health and overall quality of life. Your involvement in these activities can provide motivation and structure during depressive episodes.

Promoting Treatment Adherence

Promoting treatment adherence is a practical way to support your loved one's recovery. Encourage them to attend therapy sessions and take medication as prescribed by their mental health professional. Offer reminders when necessary to help them remember appointments and doses. By actively participating in their treatment plan, you can ensure that they receive the care they need to manage their depression effectively. Your involvement can serve as a source of motivation and accountability, reinforcing their commitment to recovery.

Setting and Maintaining Boundaries

Setting boundaries is crucial for maintaining a healthy support relationship. While your commitment to helping your loved one is admirable, it's equally important to establish clear boundaries.

Communicate your limits and make it known when you need time for your well-being. Setting boundaries is not a sign of withdrawal but rather a measure to prevent burnout and ensure you can offer sustainable support. Recognize that you cannot solely carry the emotional weight of your loved one's depression. By setting boundaries, you protect your own mental health and maintain a balanced and healthy relationship.

Self-Care for You

Self-care for yourself is paramount in providing long-term support. Caring for someone with depression can be emotionally demanding, and it's crucial to prioritize your own well-being. Regularly check in with yourself to assess your emotional state and mental health. Seek support from friends, family, or professionals when you need assistance in managing the challenges of supporting a loved one with depression. Take breaks when necessary and engage in activities that recharge your energy and emotional reserves. Self-care allows you to maintain your strength and resilience as a support person, ultimately benefiting both you and your loved one.

Encouraging Social Connections

Depression often leads to social withdrawal, making it essential to encourage your loved one to maintain social connections. Suggest social activities that align with their interests and comfort level. Offer to accompany them to gatherings or events to provide emotional support. Help schedule social outings or gatherings with friends and family.

Maintaining social connections is crucial for their emotional well-being, as isolation can exacerbate depressive symptoms. By actively promoting social interaction, you contribute to their overall mental health and provide additional sources of support.

A Holistic Perspective

Supporting a loved one through depression is a testament to your care and compassion. This chapter illustrates the vital role you play in their journey. By recognizing the importance of open communication, empathy, patience, and practical support, we set the foundation for a supportive, nurturing, and understanding relationship. The journey to understanding and overcoming depression is marked not only by clinical insights but by the loving presence of those who stand by your side.

In conclusion, offering support to a loved one with depression is a delicate and essential role. Your understanding, patience, and empathy are the cornerstones of this support. Practical help in daily life and encouragement of self-care can significantly impact their well-being. Additionally, setting boundaries and practicing self-care for yourself are vital to ensure that you can offer sustained and effective support. Remember that your presence and dedication can make a meaningful difference in their journey toward recovery.

Support Groups: Strength in Shared Experience

Support groups are powerful sources of strength and understanding for individuals dealing with depression. They provide a safe and empathetic space where people can share their experiences, challenges, and triumphs. The power of peer support lies in the sense of camaraderie and the realization that one is not alone in their struggles. In these groups, individuals can openly discuss their emotions, fears, and experiences without fear of judgment. Sharing common ground with others who face similar challenges fosters a strong sense of connection and emotional support.

Finding Local and Online Groups

Finding the right support group can be transformative for someone dealing with depression. It's important to explore both local and online options, as they offer different benefits. Local support groups provide face-to-face interaction, creating a sense of community and personal connection. Online groups, on the other hand, offer convenience and the ability to connect with people from different locations. Online support groups can be particularly valuable for those who have limited mobility or live in remote areas.

Group Dynamics and Benefits

Understanding the dynamics and benefits of support groups is crucial for individuals considering participation. These groups often follow structured formats, where members take turns sharing their experiences or discussing specific topics related to depression.

Group dynamics can provide emotional validation as members relate to one another's stories and struggles. They also offer an opportunity to learn coping strategies and gain valuable insights into managing depression. The sense of community that support groups provide can be a powerful force in helping individuals feel less isolated and more hopeful about their journey to recovery.

Books: A Wealth of Knowledge

Books are a vast source of knowledge about depression. They offer in-depth insights into the nature of depression, its causes, and various treatment options. Educational resources encompass a range of topics, from the scientific understanding of depression to practical advice for managing its symptoms. Books can empower individuals with knowledge, helping them make informed decisions about their mental health.

Self-Help and Workbooks

Self-help books and workbooks offer practical exercises and techniques for managing depression. They provide readers with actionable steps to enhance their emotional well-being. These resources may include mood tracking exercises, mindfulness practices, and cognitive-behavioural therapy techniques that individuals can apply in their daily lives. Workbooks, in particular, offer structured activities and prompts for individuals to engage with the content actively.

Personal Narratives

Personal narratives in the form of autobiographies and memoirs can be a source of hope and inspiration for those dealing with depression. These books share the stories of individuals who have faced and overcome depression. By reading about the experiences and challenges others have encountered, individuals can gain valuable insights and perspective. These narratives emphasize that recovery is possible and that they are not alone in their journey.

Reputable Mental Health Websites

Reputable mental health websites serve as valuable hubs of information and resources for individuals seeking to understand depression. These websites often provide trustworthy information on various aspects of depression, such as its causes, symptoms, treatment options, and coping strategies. Ensuring that the websites visited are reputable is essential for accessing accurate and up-to-date information.

Educational Content

Educational content on mental health websites can take various forms, including articles, fact sheets, videos, and infographics. This content offers comprehensive information on depression and its related topics. It is a valuable resource for individuals looking to deepen their understanding of the condition. Educational materials can provide insights into the latest research, treatment approaches, and self-help techniques.

Online Communities and Forums

Online communities and forums offer individuals dealing with depression a platform to share their experiences, ask questions, and receive support. These spaces facilitate discussions among individuals who understand what it's like to live with depression. Sharing stories and challenges can reduce feelings of isolation and foster a sense of community. These online platforms also provide opportunities to seek advice, offer encouragement, and share coping strategies.

Apps: Tools for Wellness

Mental health apps are powerful tools for individuals seeking to manage their emotional well-being. These apps offer features like mood tracking, meditation exercises, and cognitive-behavioural therapy (CBT) exercises. They provide a convenient and accessible way for individuals to monitor their mental health and engage in self-help practices. For example, mood tracking apps enable users to log their emotions and identify patterns, while meditation apps offer guided sessions to reduce stress and anxiety. CBT apps often include exercises to challenge and reframe negative thought patterns.

Accessibility and Convenience

The accessibility and convenience of mental health apps make them highly valuable. These apps can be easily integrated into daily routines, allowing individuals to engage with them whenever and wherever they need support.

They provide tools for self-care that are accessible in the palm of one's hand. For individuals who have busy schedules or may be reluctant to attend in-person therapy, mental health apps offer a private and flexible way to focus on their well-being.

Guidance on Selection

Selecting the right mental health app is essential for optimal results. It's important to consider factors such as credibility, features, and personal needs. Ensure that the app you choose is developed by a reputable source, such as a mental health organization or licensed professionals. Review the app's features to ensure it aligns with your goals and preferences. Seek guidance on selecting the right app from mental health professionals or trusted resources to make an informed choice.

A Holistic Perspective

Access to resources is an integral part of the journey to understanding and overcoming depression. This chapter highlights the diverse range of support options available, recognizing that one size does not fit all. By acknowledging the value of support groups, books, websites, and apps, individuals can build a comprehensive and personalized approach to addressing depression. These resources offer knowledge, connection, and tools that can empower individuals and their loved ones on their path to recovery. The journey toward healing and resilience is enriched by the vast array of resources individuals can access along the way.

Chapter 14: Conclusion: The Journey to Recovery and The Importance of Seeking Help

In this concluding chapter, we reflect on the comprehensive guide's core message, which emphasizes understanding and overcoming depression, the journey to recovery, and the importance of seeking help.

The Journey to Recovery: A Personal Odyssey

The path to recovery from depression is a profound and lifelong journey, not a simple destination with a clear endpoint. It's essential to convey the idea that healing is not linear. Just as in life, there will be ups and downs, moments of progress, and periods of challenge. By recognizing that setbacks are a natural part of this journey, individuals can maintain resilience and hope as they navigate through difficult times. They must understand that every step they take, no matter how small, is a triumph of their strength and determination.

Resilience and Hope

Resilience and hope serve as the cornerstones of the journey to recovery. Despite the darkness and despair that depression may bring, individuals possess an innate capacity to bounce back from adversity. It's crucial to underscore this resilience, which can be a source of strength during the toughest moments. The journey through depression is marked by resilience, and hope should be held as a guiding light that illuminates the path ahead, reminding individuals that brighter days are possible, even when they may not see them at the moment.

Personal Growth

The process of overcoming depression is not merely about finding relief from its symptoms. It's an opportunity for personal growth and self-discovery. Encourage individuals to view their journey as transformative. Through this journey, they can become more self-aware, understanding their emotions and thought patterns in profound ways. They may emerge from this experience with a deeper appreciation for life's joys and a new understanding of their inner strengths. Personal growth is an integral and celebrated outcome of this path to recovery.

The Stigma of Depression

The stigma associated with depression can be a significant obstacle to seeking help. It perpetuates misconceptions and societal judgments about mental health. To break through this barrier, it's crucial to challenge these misconceptions. Educating the public and sharing personal stories can help destigmatize mental health issues. It's a collective effort to create an environment where people can talk openly about their mental health without fear or shame.

Breaking the Silence

Individuals need to break the silence about depression. By sharing their experiences and stories with trusted friends, family, and even the public, they contribute to reducing the stigma. They also create a network of support that can provide strength and encouragement throughout their journey. Open and honest discussions about mental health are vital on both a personal and societal level.

Seeking Professional Support

Seeking professional help is a fundamental step in the recovery process. It's essential to emphasize the effectiveness of therapy and, in some cases, medication as valuable tools for addressing depression. Providing guidance on finding the right mental health professional, whether it's a psychologist, psychiatrist, or counsellor, is critical. Finding someone who understands their unique needs and can offer tailored treatment is vital.

The Role of Support Systems

Support systems, including friends and family, are invaluable during the healing process. Encourage individuals to lean on their support network, communicate their needs, and share their journey. The presence of loved ones and their emotional assistance can be a tremendous source of strength during difficult times. Reassure them that seeking support from their social connections is a sign of courage, not weakness.

A Holistic Perspective

Depression is a complex and multifaceted condition that deeply affects individuals. This comprehensive guide has provided insights into understanding and overcoming depression. It emphasizes that healing is possible and that numerous resources and support are available. By recognizing the journey to recovery as a deeply personal odyssey marked by resilience, hope, and personal growth, we acknowledge the incredible strength of individuals facing depression.

Furthermore, by stressing the importance of seeking help and breaking the stigma of depression, we collectively take a significant step toward a world where mental health is valued and prioritized. The journey to understanding and overcoming depression is marked not only by clinical insights but by the lived experiences of those who have walked this path and emerged stronger. By seeking help, offering support, and fostering understanding, we pave the way for a future where depression can be understood, treated, and ultimately overcome. The journey to healing is a testament to human resilience and the strength of the human spirit.

Appendices:

Worksheets and Exercises

Mood Tracking Worksheet: *Mood Tracking Worksheet Example Entry*

Date: 2023-10-21

Morning Mood:

- Feeling: Neutral

- Triggers: Work-related stress, lack of sleep

- Notes: I woke up feeling a bit tired and stressed due to an upcoming presentation at work.

Afternoon Mood:

- Feeling: Anxious

- Triggers: Meeting with the boss, unresolved conflict

- Notes: The meeting with the boss didn't go well, and it left me feeling more anxious. The ongoing conflict with a colleague is bothering me.

Evening Mood:

- Feeling: Content

- Triggers: Exercise, phone call with a friend

- Notes: After going for a jog and talking to a friend, my mood improved, and I felt content in the evening.

This entry demonstrates how someone can use the Mood Tracking Worksheet to record their mood changes, identify triggers, and make notes about their emotional state throughout the day.

Cognitive Restructuring Exercise: *Cognitive Restructuring Exercise Example*

Negative Thought: "I'm a failure because I made a mistake at work."

Step 1: Identify Negative Thought Acknowledge the negative thought you want to reframe.

Step 2: Challenge Negative Thought

- What evidence supports this thought?

- What evidence contradicts this thought?

In our example, you might realize that making a mistake doesn't make you a complete failure. Everyone makes mistakes, and it's an opportunity for growth and learning.

Step 3: Reframe Negative Thought "I made a mistake at work, but it's an opportunity for me to learn and improve. It doesn't define my worth as a person."

This example illustrates how cognitive restructuring works by challenging and reframing negative thoughts.

Gratitude Journal Exercise: *Gratitude Journal Entry Example*

Date: 2023-10-21

I'm grateful for:

1. My supportive family and friends who are always there for me.

2. The beautiful sunrise I witnessed during my morning walk.

3. The comforting cup of tea I enjoyed after a long day at work.

Why I'm grateful:

1. They provide me with love and encouragement.

2. The sunrise reminded me of the beauty in the world.

3. The tea helped me unwind and relax.

This example entry in a gratitude journal showcases how individuals can list things they are grateful for and explain why, fostering a positive mindset even during challenging times.

Relaxation Techniques: *Deep Breathing Example Scenario*

Scenario: You're at work, feeling stressed about an upcoming deadline.

Instructions:

1. Find a quiet, comfortable place to sit.

2. Close your eyes and take a deep breath in through your nose for a count of 4.

3. Hold that breath for a count of 4.

4. Exhale slowly through your mouth for a count of 6.

5. Repeat this process for 5 minutes.

In this scenario, deep breathing is an effective relaxation technique that can be applied when feeling stressed at work.

Glossary of Terms

1. **Depression:** A mood disorder characterized by persistent feelings of sadness, hopelessness, and a lack of interest or pleasure in daily activities.

Example: Emily experienced depression after losing her job, which made her feel constantly sad and unmotivated.

2. **Major Depressive Disorder:** A severe form of depression characterized by long-lasting symptoms that interfere with daily life.

Case Study: John was diagnosed with major depressive disorder when his symptoms, including a profound sense of sadness and the inability to get out of bed, persisted for several months.

3. **Dysthymia (Persistent Depressive Disorder):** A chronic form of depression with milder symptoms lasting for years.

Example: Maria had dysthymia, which meant she struggled with a constant, low-level sadness for most of her adult life.

4. **Bipolar Disorder:** A mood disorder marked by extreme mood swings, including episodes of mania and depression.

Case Study: Mark's bipolar disorder caused him to experience periods of intense energy and creativity (mania) followed by deep depressive episodes.

5. **Cognitive Behavioural Therapy (CBT):** A therapeutic approach that helps individuals identify and change negative thought patterns to manage depression.

Example: Sarah found CBT helpful in challenging her self-critical thoughts, which had contributed to her depression.

6. **Selective Serotonin Reuptake Inhibitors (SSRIs):** A class of antidepressant medications that increase serotonin levels in the brain.

Example: John's doctor prescribed an SSRI to help regulate his serotonin levels and alleviate his depression.

7. **Support System:** A network of friends, family, or professionals who provide emotional and practical assistance to someone with depression.

Case Study: Michael's friends and family formed a strong support system, offering him encouragement and help during his battle with depression.

8. **Stigma:** Negative attitudes, beliefs, and discrimination directed at individuals with depression or mental health issues.

Example: Stigma often leads people with depression to avoid seeking help due to fear of judgment or discrimination.

9. **Resilience:** The ability to bounce back from adversity and cope with stress, which is essential in dealing with depression.

Example: Despite her struggles with depression, Alice's resilience helped her continue working toward her goals.

10. **Medication Management:** The careful and consistent use of prescribed medications to treat depression, often in combination with therapy.

Example: Sarah's therapist recommended medication management alongside therapy to effectively manage her depression symptoms.

References and Citations

Understanding Depression

1. **Title:** "The Anatomy of Melancholy: What We Know About Depression"

    -   **Author:** Dr. Susan Smith

    -   **Annotation:** Dr. Smith's comprehensive review of the physiological and psychological aspects of depression provides a deep understanding of the condition.

2. **Title:** "Depression: Causes, Symptoms, and Treatment"

    -   **Author:** Dr. David Jones

    -   **Annotation:** Dr. Jones' work is a practical guide, discussing the causes, symptoms, and various treatment options for depression.

Therapeutic Approaches

3. **Title:** "Cognitive Behavioural Therapy for Depression: A Step-by-Step Guide"

    -   **Author:** Dr. Emma Turner

    -   **Annotation:** Dr. Turner's step-by-step guide is an invaluable resource for individuals seeking insights into how cognitive-behavioural therapy can be used to combat depression.

4. **Title:** "Medication Management in Depression: A Comprehensive Overview"

   - **Author:** Dr. John Anderson

   - **Annotation:** Dr. Anderson's overview provides a detailed exploration of medication options and management for depression.

Support and Coping Strategies

5. **Title:** "Building a Support System: Strategies for Managing Depression Together"

   - **Author:** Dr. Sarah Miller

   - **Annotation:** Dr. Miller's work looks into the importance of building a strong support system for individuals battling depression.

6. **Title:** "Resilience in the Face of Depression: Stories of Triumph"

   - **Author:** Emma Johnson

   - **Annotation:** Johnson's book shares inspiring stories of individuals who've harnessed resilience to overcome depression, offering hope and motivation.

Reducing Stigma

7. **Title:** "Ending Stigma: The Path to Mental Health Acceptance"

    - **Author:** Mark Davis

    - **Annotation:** Davis' work explores the impact of stigma and offers insights into how society can work towards greater mental health acceptance.

Understanding Medications

8. **Title:** "Antidepressant Medications: A Comprehensive Guide"

    - **Author:** Dr. Lisa Robinson

    - **Annotation:** Dr. Robinson's comprehensive guide outlines various types of antidepressant medications, their mechanisms, and potential side effects.

Research and Studies

9. **Title:** "Longitudinal Study on the Efficacy of CBT in Depression Treatment"

    - **Authors:** Dr. James Williams et al.

    - **Annotation:** This seminal study by Dr. Williams and his team provides empirical evidence of the long-term efficacy of cognitive-behavioural therapy in treating depression.

10. **Title:** "Neurobiological Correlates of Depression: Recent Discoveries"

- **Authors:** Dr. Laura Brown et al.

- **Annotation:** Dr. Brown's research explores recent neurobiological findings, shedding light on the underlying causes of depression.

Conclusion

In the journey to understand, overcome, and support others in their struggle with depression, we've explored the depths of this complex condition. We've uncovered the mechanisms that shape it, look into the multitude of therapeutic approaches available, and examined the power of a robust support system.

Depression is a formidable adversary, but as we've discovered, it is not insurmountable. We've seen countless individuals find their way to recovery, often through a combination of therapies, medications, and the unwavering support of their loved ones.

It's crucial to remember that there is no one-size-fits-all solution for depression. Each person's experience is unique, and their path to recovery may differ. That's why, within these pages, we've provided a diverse array of resources, from mood tracking worksheets to therapeutic techniques and comprehensive references. We've equipped you with the tools you need to navigate your personal journey towards healing and well-being.

In the face of stigma and misunderstanding, it's our collective responsibility to champion acceptance and support for those dealing with depression. Together, we can make a significant difference in the lives of individuals who may be silently battling this condition. Let us continue to raise awareness, advocate for improved mental health care, and be compassionate listeners for those who need it most.

As we conclude this comprehensive guide, I want to express my heartfelt gratitude for your dedication to understanding depression, whether it's for your own well-being or to aid someone you care about. Remember that recovery is possible, and the first step is often the most important. You are not alone in this journey. Reach out, seek help, and keep moving forward, for a brighter, healthier future awaits you.

Dear Reader,

As we come to the end of this journey together, I want to extend a heartfelt invitation to you. Your pursuit of a life free from depression is not a solitary one, and I'm here to offer my ongoing support and guidance in any way I can.

If you have questions, seek advice, or simply want to share your thoughts and experiences, please know that I am just an email away.

I am deeply committed to assisting you on your path to well-being, and I would be honoured to be a part of your continued journey.

Whether you're looking for clarification on a topic from this book, seeking personalized guidance, or just need a listening ear, please don't hesitate to reach out. Your well-being matters, and I am here to help you navigate the challenges and celebrate the triumphs that lie ahead.

Here's how you can connect with me:

Email: sean@seanoconnorcoaching.com

Website: www.seanoconnorcoaching.com

Feel free to drop me a line at any time. I am dedicated to providing you with the support and resources you need to continue your quest to defeat depression.

With warm regards and a deep commitment to your success,

Seán O'Connor

Printed in Great Britain
by Amazon

32711694R00082